Fearless Love

Anne Sanderson

D1421498

Christian Focus

This book has been written
with appreciation for the
ministry and support of
Rev. Guy R. Finnie

For a free catalogue of all our titles, please write to
Christian Focus Publications,
Geanies House, Fearn,
Ross-shire, IV20 1TW, Great Britain

For details of our titles visit us on our web site
http://www.christianfocus.com

ISBN 1 85792 506 8

Published in 2000 by Christian Focus Publications,
Geanies House, Fearn, Ross-shire,
IV20 1TW, Great Britain

Cover design by Owen Daily

Contents

Introduction

Not many people like to see Jehovah's Witnesses (JWs) walk up the garden path. Two robbers in the middle of attacking a poor woman in a remote cottage were so frightened by just such an event, they dropped their axe and fled rather than open the door! However, the much relieved householder succinctly summed it up when she said, 'I am probably the only woman in Britain happy to hear the Jehovah's Witnesses at the door!' [1]

Hopefully, the next time JWs call you will not be in such dire straits. Yet you will probably be just as unprepared as those robbers were, wishing to make a hasty departure rather than have to face the JWs' doorstep sermon.

The good news is, you *can* face them with confidence. You do not have to run away or hide behind feeble excuses any more. There *is* a loving way to answer JWs which will not only enable you to act in a commendably Christian manner but might also help release them from the deception and the fear which binds them.

The not-so-good news is that there is no set formula for such a response. You cannot read a word-for-word script, memorise and repeat it verbatim. Learning to help JWs is no easy task. I should know. For the many years I was a JW I gave Christians a hard time whenever they tried to help me. But thanks to the fearless love several Christians showed me over a prolonged period the shoe is now on the other foot. I am dedicated to helping JWs. There are hundreds of Christians engaged in this task, resulting in thousands of Witnesses entering into 'the glorious freedom of the children of God' (Rom. 8:21).

Sadly, our efforts are often misunderstood by the ones we are trying to help. We have been accused both verbally and in writing of envy, spite and even Satanic possession. I have in my files letters from JWs to former members and to Christians who have never been Witnesses saying such things as, 'You are a heretic, blasphemer and disciple of the shining one. At Armageddon you and your fellow ex-members will be hanged by the sinews of your body and your tongues torn out and thrown into Sheol.... We will not be converted into false creeds by Satanic fornicants.' Also, 'We have been warned about you and your friend! If you don't keep away from our members then we will take drastic action and you will regret it! You can't win, we will drive you into the ground. Jehovah will send us protection from Heaven. Stop now before it's too late. You are doing the work of Satan. You are the whore of Babylon! You are the devil incarnate – back to the pit, you stinking vomit.... I'm not signing this – so you will never know who it's from. 666 – you.'

Certainly, we don't reach out to JWs for the sake of popularity! We do it because we love them. We believe them to be sincere, but sincerely wrong. If only they can be persuaded to stop looking at their Watch Tower Society long enough to consider who Jesus is, then they might realise their need to turn to him instead of an organisation. Christ liberates people into the glorious freedom of the sons of God. JWs do not know what that freedom is. They cannot experience it because of their bondage to this organisation, and their chances of ever discovering such liberation whilst remaining JWs are so remote that some Christians endeavour to help lead them along the road to Christian freedom.

It is by no means an entirely thankless task. Underneath the apparently unruffled surface of the massive Watch Tower organisation are thousands of deeply distressed individuals in turmoil. The advent of the Internet has disclosed great disquiet and unhappiness at having to toe the Society line. Particularly in America there are groups, some even set up by JWs (but anonymously because otherwise they would be thrown out), seeking reform within the Society, whilst others have broken away and set up splinter groups. Browsing through their web-sites is an education. Although it can be heart-breaking, it is very encouraging to learn that there are thinking people amongst Witnesses who object to injustice and totalitarian regimentation. Very many JWs have been enabled to break free through making contact with like-minded individuals and Christian ministries on the Net. Jesus' command to become fishers of men is having an exciting application amongst those fishing with this particular 'Net'! The potential catch of seeking JWs is great, and the Society knows it. Despite warning Witnesses not to surf the Net in such areas, and disfellowshiping those it discovers disregarding their attempts at control,[2] an exodus has begun. There always was a steady turnover of members, but now the trickle is becoming a stream, and with impending doctrinal changes in process, there could soon be a flood of disillusioned JWs.

The problem is, who will be there to help them find the courage to leave, and to offer direction when they do? The majority of Christians are in no position to do so because they neither care nor grasp what is involved in trying to leave. There is also the problem of keeping up to date with Society teaching and methods; unless Christians can use the Internet or have subscribed to a specialist Christian ministry, current information will pass them by and they will be unaware of the latest 'revealed truth' dazzling JWs. There is a great need for up-to-date information.

I hope this book is more than a manual on 'How to help JWs'. Because it is primarily concerned with '*Why* help JWs?' it is designed to motivate the Body of Christ into practical action when God-given opportunities arise in the form of uninvited Witnesses on the doorstep. It aims to touch Christians' hearts with the principle of Paul's plea for his own race: 'Brethren, my heart's desire and prayer to God for Israel is that they may be saved. For I bear them witness that they have a zeal for God, but not according to knowledge' (Rom 10:1,2 NKJV). My heart's desire and prayer to God for the JWs is that they may be saved. For I can bear witness that they are zealous for God, but their zeal is not according to divine knowledge. They have sought to establish their own righteousness instead of submitting to God's righteousness in Christ. But how can they call on the one in whom they have not believed? Although they have heard of him, they have heard a distorted message, a different gospel, which is no gospel at all. Paul's words apply perfectly, 'turning to a different gospel – which is really no gospel at all.

Evidently some people are throwing you into confusion and are trying to pervert the gospel of Christ' (Gal. 1:6b-7). Faith comes from hearing the message of the gospel about Christ. Who will be bold enough to compare their distorted gospel with the true gospel? Only those whose heart's desire and prayer to God is that the JWs may be saved.

To touch your hearts, I quote a poem composed by Ella, who was baptised as a Christian in 1988. She wrote her testimony in verse. It captures the essence of so many people who, struggling in an effort to find Christ, are beguiled by the JWs before joyfully finding Christ at last:

When I was about twenty-four,
A Jehovah's Witness knocked at my door.
One week before to the day,
On bended knees I'd asked the way.
I thought, this is the answer to my prayer,
That is why she's standing there.

In her hand was God's own book,
I said that I would take a look.
'Come in, come in, and have some tea,
And tell me what God wants of me.'
Every week she'd come to teach,
Every week she'd come to preach.

Then every Sunday she would call
To take me to the Kingdom Hall.
Five meetings they had every week,
Fed on 'Watchtower' spiritual meat.
No crown of glory for your head;
Well, that is what 'The Watchtower' said.

The promise of heaven is not for you,
That's just for the chosen few.
I believed all they said;
Faith without works is dead.
So out door knocking I would go,
Selling 'Watchtowers' to and fro.

'This is the truth!' I'd tell them all,
'Come with me to the Kingdom Hall.'
'The end is near,' I would cry,
'Join our ranks, or you will die!'

My days were joyless, full of dread
Because of what 'The Watchtower' said.
'Is this the way?' I began to ponder,
'Is this the truth?' I began to wonder.
For loyalties sake I thought along,
'They must be right; it's me who's wrong.'

I searched and looked but couldn't find,
I didn't know then that I was blind;
Blind to God's saving grace,
Forgiveness for the human race.
There was no joy, there was no peace,
The search for God began to cease.

The Watchtower's yoke wasn't light,
I gave it back and then took flight.
Finally, I drew away,
But lived in fear of Judgment Day,
Until one day a gate I passed,
And the man there said, 'Hello!'

He asked, 'Have you been saved, my dear?
Are you truly born again?'
I really didn't want to know;
I nearly told him where to go!

You see, I was taught not to speak
To a Pentecostal freak!
At first I was horrified,
They spoke in tongues and prophesied.
My way was right, he was wrong;
I'd change his mind before too long.

I met his wife soon after that
And many times would have a chat.
'Come in,' she said, 'There's tea for two.
I know just what God wants for you.'
Hard going it was on their part.
Through this, all others please take heart.

The way to God was to repent,
Confess my sins and relent.
'Forgive me, Lord,' I asked one day,
And Jesus washed my sins away.
The Watchtower's lies had blinded me,
But God's Holy Spirit made me see.

At last I found faith, hope and love,
Put in my heart by God above.
Lastly, I can't say exactly when,
But now I know I'm born again.

This poem will never receive literary acclaim, but I applaud it as a fine account of how JW influence can be overcome, and why it *needs* to be overcome. How many more Ellas are there, people who have asked God to show them the way, only to have Witnesses knock at their door? How many are there who find no peace or joy in the Watch Tower Society but do not know where else to go?

Who will speak the truth in love to them? Will

you? To do that you need to know the truth and have godly love. Bearing in mind Christianity is not a head-trip but a heart transplant, outreach to Witnesses must begin with love, continue in love, and finish with love. Any lack a Christian might have in knowledge will be more than made up for by godly love. Some of the most effective outreaches have been where a few simple, loving words were said, or a kindly action done.

To start unravelling error from truth and to counter fear with love, let us look carefully at JWs, then at ourselves, and see what can be done. This exercise will not take us along the route normally mapped out by writers on the subject. Such pathways can be like jungle tracks hacked out of dense, dark tangles of theology and many able theologians have already cleared the way in that regard, particularly with such doctrines as the Trinity, the soul, hell, etc. Occasionally, however, I take a side-swipe at a little 'spiritual undergrowth' which has been neglected!

My intention is to take you on a mystery tour, revealing to you what makes JWs what they are and why they think and act as they do. I also want to give you a glimpse of the tortuous track to liberation from the Watch Tower Society. But the excursion will also take us inside the Christian Church, to examine fears, prejudices and lack of love sometimes found there. Throughout, our way will be signposted by scripture, so have your Bible ready.

We will start our mystery tour by trying to understand what JWs make of certain passages of scripture which lead them 180 degrees away from the Christian Church, the Body of Christ. If ever we are to help them, it is vital we understand why they feel revulsion at what, to us, is our cherished inheritance in Christ. After taking this route, I hope you, too, will be filled with a fearless love for JWs which will enable you to 'speak the truth in love' to them (Eph. 4:15). There are very many texts about love which could help us, but perhaps the most appropriate one is in 1 John 4:17-19:

> In this way, love is made complete among us so that we will have confidence on the day of judgment, because in this world we are like him. There is no fear in love. But perfect love drives out fear, because fear has to do with punishment. The one who fears is not made perfect in love. We love because he first loved us.

As the book progresses, the impact of this particular text should become clear.

Anne Sanderson
Larbert,
Scotland

Chapter 1

Them and Us

To understand Jehovah's Witnesses, you need to be able to see the world through their spectacles which are definitely not rose-tinted! Their attitudes and understanding have been created by particular interpretations of particular scriptures.

The fundamental interpretation which is the most important for Christians to understand is that of Matthew 24:45-51: 'Who then is a faithful and wise servant, whom his master made ruler over his household, to give them food in due season? Blessed is that servant whom his master, when he comes, will find so doing. Assuredly, I say to you that he will make him ruler over all his goods. But if that evil servant says in his heart, "My master is delaying his coming," and begins to beat his fellow servants, and to eat and drink with the drunkards, the master of that servant will come on a day when he is not looking for him and at an hour that he is not aware of, and will cut him in two and appoint him his portion with the hypocrites. There shall be weeping and gnashing of teeth' (NKJV).

The key to JW authority
The JW Bible (the *New World Translation* – NWT) renders 'a faithful and wise servant' as 'the faithful and discreet slave' (the phrase used throughout here). If the JW interpretation of this passage is inaccurate,

13

their entire worldview disintegrates for it is founded on deception. There is *nothing* more important to the Watch Tower Bible and Tract Society than this text, upon which it bases its immense authority.

The Watch Tower Society maintains that today there is a small core of JWs who comprise this faithful and discreet slave class. *All* of the members of this class are JWs. They are all, they believe, anointed with God's holy spirit (but because they deny his personality, they always use the lower case: God's holy spirit, which will be so written in this book whenever used in a JW context). And they see them as the only ones whom God is using to give spiritual food to Christians today. According to JW teaching they were found to be faithful when Christ inspected all religions in 1919 – they were lovingly, obediently caring for the things of Christ. None of the clergy of Christendom were, according to the Society. *They* were supporting war and not proclaiming the good news that God's kingdom had been established in 1914. So, when Jesus examined the world in 1919, he decided that only JWs were fit to be called his people. He gave the leaders of the Watch Tower Society the responsibility of being in charge of *all* of Christ's 'possessions'. [1]

Anyone who wanted spiritual nourishment would have to go to them – and them alone. The whole world would suffer spiritual famine, but spiritual plenty would be freely available to all who meekly submitted to the authority of the Watch Tower Society.

'...Jehovah's organization alone, in all the earth, is directed by God's holy spirit or active force.... Only

14

this organization functions for Jehovah's purpose and to his praise. To it alone God's Sacred Word, the Bible, is not a sealed book... this organization alone is supplied with 'gifts in men,' such as evangelizers, shepherds and teachers' (*The Watchtower*, 1st July 1973, p 402). [2]

The faithful and discreet slave class is looked upon with reverential awe by all JWs. They are an elite core who are in direct communication with God. Every word they utter *must* be obeyed as if God himself were speaking. Even if a JW is convinced that something uttered by this faithful and discreet slave is wrong, he must not speak out against what has been decreed:

'We should meekly go along with the Lord's theocratic organization and wait for further clarification, rather than balk at the first mention of a thought unpalatable to us and proceed to quibble and mouth our criticisms and opinions as though they were worth more than the slave's provision of spiritual food.... After receiving these food supplies we prove their Scripturalness for ourselves to make the message our own, in a spirit of meekness and trustfulness and not combativeness' (*The Watchtower*, 1st February 1952, p 80).

Anyone who persists in voicing disagreement with the slave class is worthy of disfellowshipment – excommunication. This is what H. C. Covington, then lawyer to the Watch Tower Society in 1954, said during a Scottish court trial:

Q Unity at all costs?

A Unity at all costs, because we believe and are sure that Jehovah God is using our organisation to direct it, even though mistakes are made from time to time.

Q And unity based upon an enforced acceptance of false prophecy?

A That is conceded to be true.

Q And the person who expressed his view, as you say, that it was wrong, and was disfellowshiped, would be in breach of the Covenant, if he was baptised?

A That is correct.

Q And as you said yesterday, expressly, would be worthy of death?

A I think...

Q Would you say yes or no?

A I will answer yes, unhesitatingly. [3]

To understand why such a clearly undesirable state of affairs can be desirable to JWs we need to grasp a closely related interpretation of such passages as these:

'I have other sheep that are not of this sheep pen. I must bring them also. They too will listen to my voice, and there shall be one flock and one shepherd' (John 10:16).

'"Do not harm the land or the sea or the trees until we put a seal on the foreheads of the servants of our God." Then I heard the number of those who were sealed: 144,000 from all the tribes of Israel' (Rev. 7:3,4).

'Then I looked, and there before me was the Lamb, standing on Mount Zion, and with him 144,000 who had his name and his Father's name written on their foreheads. And I heard a sound from heaven like the roar of rushing waters and like a loud peal of thunder. The sound I heard was like that of harpists playing their harps. And they sang a new song before the throne and before the four living creatures and the elders. No-one could learn the song except the 144,000 who had been redeemed from the earth. These are those who did not defile themselves with women, for they kept themselves pure. They follow the Lamb wherever he goes. They were purchased from among men and offered as firstfruits to God and the Lamb. No lie was found in their mouths; they are blameless' (Rev. 14:1-5).

'Do not be afraid, little flock, for your Father has been pleased to give you the kingdom' (Luke 12:32).

The terms 'other sheep', 'little flock' and '144,000' are used. Anyone speaking to JWs needs to know what these terms mean to JWs and their connection with the faithful and discreet slave class. Put simply, JWs believe in a two-tier Christianity.

(a) There is an elite group, limited in number to 144,000. These comprise 'The Little Flock', or 'The Anointed' – anointed with God's holy spirit. (When referring only to the few thousand of this group alive today, they are called 'The Remnant'.)

(b) Then there is 'The Great Crowd' who are unlimited in number. They are also called 'The Other Sheep'. They are *not* anointed with God's holy spirit.

This anointing of the holy spirit is the crucial

difference between the two classes. *Only* those anointed with the holy spirit will go to heaven. Only 8,755 JWs worldwide today claim to be anointed, and over five million baptised JWs know they are *not* anointed. The 'great crowd of other sheep' know they will never go to heaven, they know they will never see Christ and they have no assurance of salvation. They hope they might be saved eventually if they prove themselves obedient to the faithful and discreet slave class. But any disloyalty to this class equals disloyalty to God. If Armageddon, God's war against the wicked, comes whilst they are being disloyal, they will die, never to be resurrected.

Now it becomes clear why JWs will go along with something they personally disbelieve if the faithful and discreet slave class insist it must be believed. The responsibility for maintaining spiritual truth is not entrusted to the second-class JWs; that is the task of the first-class JWs, the anointed. If they make a mistake, and they admit they are fallible, God will deal with them in time, and the mistake will be corrected. It would be highly presumptuous for any of the other sheep to tell the remnant they are wrong. Rather, such errors must simply be looked upon as an opportunity to show obedience and loyalty to the faithful and discreet slave class:

'...it must be observed that this "faithful and discreet slave" was never inspired, never perfect.... Things published were not perfect in the days of Charles Taze Russell... [the first president] nor were they perfect in the days of J. F. Rutherford, the succeeding president. The increasing light on God's Word as well as the facts of history have repeatedly required that adjustments of one kind or another be made down to the very present time. But let us never forget that the motives of this "slave" were always pure, unselfish.... Actually, any adjustments that have been made in understanding have furnished an opportunity for those being served by this "slave" to show loyalty and love.... For those who truly love God's law there is no stumbling block' (*The Watchtower*, 1st March 1977, paragraph 15 of the article 'To Whom Shall We Go But Jesus Christ').

So the Watch Tower Society has given itself the green light to change any or all doctrines it likes, knowing it will still have over five million followers loyally applauding every book and magazine printed, enthusiastically exclaiming delight at the newest 'revealed truth'. Such is the power of the slave class.

The best way to understand this two-tier Christianity is to observe what happens once every year when JWs remember Christ's death. They call this event 'The Memorial'. It is the single most important date in the JW calendar. A careful count is made of all who attend and the number who partake of the unleavened bread and the wine. In 1999 there were 14,088,751 in attendance but only 8,755 took the bread and wine. With 89,985 congregations worldwide, and many of the remnant based at Society headquarters in New York, this means that there are very many congregations where *not one single JW believes himself to be anointed with the holy spirit!* In such cases, the plate and the cup are simply passed from one person to the next, with no-one partaking, for only the anointed may partake.

This annual celebration is a very good way of illustrating the shocking need of these millions of people. They have not had their sin disposed of. They have been deceived into believing that they are still Christians, that they will meet with God's approval and be given eternal life on a paradise earth. They believe that the only genuinely spirit-anointed Christians in the world are all JWs, a tiny core of which claim to be the faithful and discreet slave class today.

One reader of *The Watchtower* magazine asked: 'Is Jesus the 'mediator' only for anointed Christians?' The answer given was: '...in this strict Biblical sense Jesus is the 'mediator' only for anointed Christians. The new covenant will terminate with the glorification of the remnant who are today in that covenant mediated by Christ. The 'great crowd' of 'other sheep' that is forming today is not in that new covenant' (1st April, 1979, p 31).

Jesus told Nicodemus that if he wanted to see God's kingdom and to be in that kingdom, he had to be 'born again'. Jesus' words, 'You must be born again' (John 3:7), are not subject to interpretation. The NWT renders Exodus 20:14 as, 'You must not commit adultery.' No JW would try to argue that this emphatic command should be applied literally to one group of believers but not to another. Yet the Watch Tower Society has attempted to force just such an interpretation on Jesus' command, 'You must be born again.'

In an article entitled 'Who Are "Born Again"?' the Society admits: 'Since Jesus Christ made the point that this was a prerequisite for entering the Kingdom of God, it is vital that we do understand what he meant by being "born again".' They explain that Jesus' disciples were born again, thereby obtaining a clean standing before God as the merits of Jesus' sacrifice were applied on their behalf. They became God's sons, accepted as part of God's family. Then they insert their interpretation of Revelation 7:4 and 14:1-3 about the 144,000, implying that this is the limited number of God's spiritual sons.

But their next statement is astounding: 'Does this mean then that in order to gain God's favor, everyone must be "born again"? Not at all.' To justify this outright contradiction of Jesus' words, they try to show that born again believers will 'enter into the [heavenly] kingdom of God' (square brackets the Society's). By adding the word 'heavenly', they are trying to make a difference between going to heaven to be in the kingdom there, and staying on earth to be part of the millennial kingdom rule believed to occur after Armageddon (*Awake!* 8th February, 1988).

Believing the word of God is something JWs cannot do when God's word contradicts any of their doctrines. John 1:12-13 says, 'But to all who received him [Jesus], who believed in his name, he gave power to become children of God; who were born, not of blood nor of the will of the flesh nor of the will of man, but of God' (RSV). All JWs would claim to have 'received' Jesus in faith, and to believe in his name. Yet less than nine thousand of them claim to have taken the power (or right) to become children of God to themselves. What is worse, a small core of this number are trying to prevent their fellow five million baptised believers from exercising this power, or taking this right. They have told them they do not have this right saying that 'all' does *not* mean 'all'; it means 144,000. Instead of believing the promises of God, they have interpreted them to mean something else. To squash his worries, a JW reading such an interpretation and doubting its accuracy will only remind himself that the writers have the holy spirit's indwelling whilst he does not.

We have seen that only a tiny percentage of JWs are responsible for forming doctrine and interpreting scripture.[4] In theory, this elite core could say anything they liked and their every word would be believed. They have told the other sheep that they are not in the covenant for a kingdom and that they *cannot expect* to be born again. As a result, the other sheep remain outside the kingdom and the new birth experience. And that is where they will stay until they realise this 'faithful and discreet slave' class has deceived them!

There is a fear element in all of this. The other sheep are fearful of being disloyal to the remnant and of the consequences of disagreeing with them. (See section on disfellowshiping to understand just how frightening some of those consequences can be.) Yet the one thing which they *should* be fearful of - namely, being prevented from entering into the kingdom of God – they do *not* fear! They have been told they will enjoy seeing the earthly aspects of God's kingdom; they are *not* barred from the kingdom. True, they will never enjoy the *heavenly* kingdom, but that is no great loss when human perfection on a paradise earth is the supposed alternative.

Now that we understand something of their hierarchical system and the subjective, unquestioning loyalty of the majority, we can go on to look at their view of everyone outside the Watch Tower Society.

The outsiders
JWs think that the only spirit-filled Christians in the world are *all* JWs. This needs some explanation, for although it may be transparently clear to a Christian that he is Spirit-filled, it is not that simple to the JW.

In Matthew 24:45-51 Jesus returns to find his servant faithfully overseeing the feeding of his fellow servants. The JWs now interpret this as applying to the years 1914 to 1919.[5] In 1914, they say, Christ invisibly returned to earth. In 1918, after examining all those who claimed to be his servants, he found only the anointed class of the JWs dutifully caring for their fellow servants. The clergy of Christendom fitted the description of a 'wicked servant' and was 'thrown out' of God's service:

'...we have been living in the period called "the conclusion of the system of things" since... the early autumn of 1914. So this "faithful and discreet slave" of the Lord Jesus Christ should be today on the scene, visibly active in his appointed service. But where? Not in any part of Christendom with its thousand or more sects, large and small, all professing to be Christian. An honest search according to the entire Word of God will discover this "slave" among the Christian witnesses of Jehovah. Since the year 1919 in particular you will find this "slave" giving out to the "domestics" of the Lord Jesus Christ their spiritual food at the proper time. This "faithful and discreet slave" is not an individual Christian man. He is a class or group or congregation' (*Life Everlasting in Freedom of the Sons of God*, pp 182, 183). [6]

So, the only place where God's approval is to be found on earth is in the Watch Tower Society, particularly the governing body:

'This worldwide care of the Kingdom interests is being carried on under the supervision of 95 branch offices of the Watch Tower Bible & Tract Society of Pennsylvania, with which the governing body of Jehovah's Christian witnesses is connected' (*Ibid*, p 186).

None of the clergy are approved by God. They are hypocrites and wicked like 'the burst open figs that cannot be eaten for badness' (*Watchtower*, 1st November 1979, p. 26 and repeated in *Watchtower* 1st March 1994, p. 16). If you associate with the clergy of Christendom you will receive only spiritual crumbs, if anything at all. JWs interpret the whore of Revelation – Babylon the Great – to mean all religion other than their own, but the most reprehensible part of this conglomerate are the clergy of Christendom. And the single, worst crime the clergy commit is the persecution of JWs!

'...the remnant of the seed of God's woman were once captive in Babylon. There, like the Israelites, they were contaminated with the Babylonian religion and systems of this world, including apostate

Christendom.... But how the clerical "rich man" class of Protestantism, Catholicism and Judaism have hated, misrepresented and fought against this liberation movement of Jehovah's remnant of the seed!... So again the Serpent stirred up his religious seed to spit out their venom of murderous hatred against the remnant on earth, the associates of the great Seed of God's woman' (*What Has Religion Done For Mankind?* pp. 307, 308, 309).

Much of a newer book, *Babylon The Great Has Fallen*, is devoted to condemning the clergy of Christendom. Why is so little said, by comparison, of other world faiths? They have been so clearly deceived by the devil, they are more to be pitied than anything else. The devil has got them believing such things as reincarnation, and they all have their triads of gods. In fact, the moment a trinity of gods is spotted by JWs, they immediately exclaim, 'Ah ha! The devil's religion!' The Trinity of Christianity is, they think, the hallmark of Satan. But because Christendom has the Bible and claims to have the Holy Spirit, its error is unpardonable.

By classifying *all* religion apart from its own as being of the devil, the Watch Tower Society has succeeded in eliminating all the 'competition'. It has spread such poison so thickly in its vast output of publishing, that no person who soaks it up for any length of time can fail to have his opinion of the Christian Church tarnished. Even his attitude toward non-Christian faiths will be damaged because he is discouraged from finding out anything about them.[7] He is therefore unable to understand the reasons why people hold to such beliefs.

The greatest damage, however, is unquestionably done to the Body of Christ, the Christian Church. By tarring *all* who say they are Christians with the same brush, be they Christians or not, they have firmly placed the 'crimes' of non-Christians on the shoulders of the Church. Therefore, if Church of England bishops are reported as saying they do not believe in the resurrection of Christ, or the virgin birth, the Watch Tower Society accuses virtually the whole of Christendom with such non-belief. If Catholic priests are reported as being practising homosexuals, then almost the whole of Christendom is depicted as tolerating gross immorality. This is no exaggeration:

> Are Christendom's clergy today any better? No, they are counterparts of those corrupt religious leaders of ancient Jerusalem.
>
> They too have rejected the Bible as God's inspired Word. In some cases they have openly labelled parts of it as 'myth'. But that is not all. Listen to just a few from among the many headlines that have appeared in the public press. From Australia: 'Minister Urges Church to Bless Homosexuals.' From New York city: 'Is Homosexuality Wicked? Episcopal Priests Say No.' From Sweden: 'Ease Sex Rule, Say Clergy.' From London: 'Bishop Wants Sex Made Legal at 14.'
>
> Their rejection of God's Messianic kingdom in the hands of his Son is also a matter of record. Like the Pharisees, Christendom's clergy have put their trust in the governments of men. They are on hand to pray when presidents and kings take office. Chaplains bless the troops as they go to war. And they are willing and eager to point to the United

Nations organization as the means by which mankind will gain the peace and security that only God's Messianic kingdom can bring.

These are only a sample of the sins that the religions of Christendom have committed. They have brought the greatest blasphemy upon the names of God and Christ, and have tried to efface true worship of Jehovah God from the earth. It is these things that make certain that Christendom's destruction is imminent (*Watchtower*, 15th January 1974, p. 52).

Because the Federal Council of Churches of Christ in America said the League of Nations was the political expression of God's kingdom on earth, *all* of Christendom has been charged with supporting this 'agency of the devil'. Compare this quotation with the one following:

'...in January of 1919 the Federal Council of Churches of Christ in America officially offered its support in writing for setting up a League of Nations and called it "the political expression of the kingdom of God on earth" ' (*Babylon The Great Has Fallen*, p. 531).

'In 1919, when *Christendom* went over to advocating and supporting the political League of Nations...' (*Then Is Finished The Mystery of God*, p. 175, italics mine).

Many examples of this could be given. I am labouring this hate campaign against the Church to show why JWs are in such fear of having anything to do with the *real* Church of Christ. They view Christendom as being so corrupt, so wicked and so evil that even if they left the Watch Tower Society they would still have nothing to do with any religion, being totally unable to distinguish between genuine, Spirit-filled Christians and those who claim to be Christians but remain unregenerate. When they *do* come across individuals who clearly demonstrate the Spirit of Christ, the only way they can cope with such a contradiction is to say that such a person will eventually become a JW! Sadly, even the most unimpeachable behaviour of Spirit-filled Christians will not convince JWs that these God-fearing individuals are in the new covenant.

The Watch Tower Society is becoming increasingly frightened of the testimony of true Christians. It has become noticeable over recent years that the homes of such Christians are no longer being visited by JWs. If you doubt this to be true, make a point of giving a clear testimony of your faith in God's salvation through Christ alone the next time they call. Invite them to visit you again. Take note of how many times they return. They may come back once, or even twice, but if you persist in claiming you have the Holy Spirit's anointing and questioning whether they do, they will stop coming. And the next time they work your street, see if your door is included in the visitation!

Recently, the Society has produced a new teaching to try to bolster confidence in their distinctly inferior portion of holy spirit. Now JWs are quick to enthuse that they, too, can have just as much of the holy spirit as anointed Christians. Notice, however, the word *'can'*. They do not say they actually have as much holy spirit as the anointed. Nor do they ever say they are anointed with the holy spirit. This is due to a recent *Watchtower* article which claims the other sheep can have equal access to the holy spirit as the anointed. It is how they apply themselves to study and prayer that will determine how much of the holy spirit they benefit from.[8] Of course, the Bible teaches that either a person is anointed with the Holy Spirit, or he is not. To say reception of the Holy Spirit's benefits is quantitatively related to the amount of study and effort one makes is to reduce the Holy Spirit to a product which can be 'bought' in greater quantities the more one works to 'purchase' it.

The Christian manner of testifying to the Holy Spirit's indwelling is therefore a mixed blessing as it has forced the Watch Tower Society to argue against such sound witness. But the Christian would have to be alert to this new teaching to expose it quickly. And, if successful in exposing it, the believer will soon find his home blacklisted. Then the people who are in the best position to reach JWs will have been identified and avoided.

However, this is not discouraging, for our confidence is in God, not JWs fear of *bona fide* Christian witness. Faithful prayer will water the seeds of truth and the fruit is in God's hands. My own conversion was the direct result of two years of faithful prayer by a Christian lady who had two discussions with me.

We have now identified three specific areas of JW fear:

(a) fear of becoming 'contaminated' by other religions, all of which are devilish,

(b) fear of criticising or leaving the Watch Tower

Society as they believe they will be annihilated at Armageddon should it begin while they are not in total agreement,

(c) and fear of Christian testimony.

Worldly contamination
Another area of fear can be mentioned. It is fear of becoming 'contaminated' by politics and commerce, i.e., 'the world'. JWs will not vote, hold political office or be employed in any area of life where they will be called upon to use weapons.[9] They are continually exhorted not to be materialistic, a sentiment with which Christians would agree, but their thinking is very different. An unmaterialistic lifestyle is applauded by JWs because they believe the entire world (i.e. everything outside the Watch Tower Society) is under the control of the devil so they should stay within the Society, undetracted by materialism, to devote as much time and energy as possible to proselytising. They consider the matter no further than that. Hence Witnesses' conscientious objection and avoidance of violence does not go so far as to prompt them to become peace-*makers* in the world or to work to eliminate the causes of poverty, or to fight against injustice or crime. They rest content at doing no violence themselves, saying that making converts to their views adds positively to peace in the world, but that is to shirk the real issues. Because their worldview is that the last days must necessarily be marked by violence, famine, war etc., culminating in Armageddon, and as they have been zealously preaching the last days and Armageddon for over 100 years, it would be contrary

to their gospel to waste time and effort trying to lessen this evidence. Their responsibility is simply to point it out.

JWs have been saying for over eighty years that the generation which was alive at the start of the first World War would see Armageddon. Now that teaching has been proved false, they are rearranging their theology to keep expectation of Armageddon high. They fail to realise that their obsession with these things prevents them performing the lifestyle God desires – to pursue justice, to love mercy, to reprove oppressors, to defend the fatherless and plead for the widows (Isa 1:17; Mic. 6:8). Yes, they are kind to their own, but because they look upon everyone and everything outside the Society as of the devil, they avoid all unnecessary contact with 'the world'.

There are two more connected fears: fear of persecution and fear of not being unique.

The idea of persecution is real enough when we consider the Bible's warning to Christians. It is clearly stated that 'everyone who wants to live a godly life in Christ Jesus will be persecuted' (2 Tim. 3:12). What is unreal in the JW estimation of persecution is the reason for its coming upon them. They say it is because they and they alone are *Jehovah's* witnesses. Isaiah 43:10 is their favourite verse: ' "You are my witnesses" is the utterance of Jehovah, "even my servant whom I have chosen".' (NWT)

The Bible, however, shows that it is the name of *Jesus* which brings about the persecution of Christians! See Matthew 5:11, Mark 10:29-30 and 13:9, Acts 9:15-16, Revelation 17:6 and 20:4.

31

Because salvation can only come from believing in the name of Jesus, (Acts 2:21, 38 and 4:12), anyone lifting up his name by word and deed will be a target for the enemy. Thousands of Christians die every year for their faith in the name of Jesus. JWs will not acknowledge that such people were persecuted because they were Christians. They do acknowledge they were persecuted for their faith, but assert that their faith was not genuine Christian faith, therefore 2 Timothy 3:12 cannot apply to them.

JWs are at great pains to emphasise their uniqueness. Delighting in being different from the churches, they are anxious to be as different as possible. No crosses or organs or collection plates in their Kingdom Halls, none of the traditional hymns or celebrations, nor any of Christendom's terminology, theology or liturgy! Even where Society theology looks orthodox it always has a twist.

Feeling they must be set apart, they are at pains to stand well away from the world. A classic example of this was the refusal of JWs to buy party political cards in Malawi in the mid 1960s. The Malawian authorities ordered all citizens to purchase a 25 cent party identification card. The Branch Office in Malawi admonished the JWs not to buy them. The result was the horrific mass persecution of Malawian JWs. Many were beaten, raped and murdered. Their homes were looted then burned. Twenty thousand fled the country, loyally adhering to what they believed was Christian principle.

Halfway round the world, Mexican JWs heard of this event with more distress than others. For many years their young men had been bribing Mexican military officials to fill out a card, called a 'cartilla', stating that they had completed a year of military instructions and were now in the first reserve of the army. All this was done with Headquarters's knowledge. Indeed, the Mexican Branch Office wrote to Headquarters about it, only to receive the reply that this was purely a matter for individual conscience. They would not be pressed further. What an example of double standards! [10] Such duplicity does not result from obeying Christ but from obeying a group of men who force on others their wrong interpretation of scripture.

Certainly, when JWs maintain the Bible's high moral standards in their personal lives they can receive ridicule and cruel treatment from ignorant people. They take this as a fulfilment of Peter's words, 'They think it strange that you do not plunge with them into the same flood of dissipation, and they heap abuse on you' (1 Pet 4:4). Although JWs are by no means unique in this regard their literature gives the impression that *only* JWs are persecuted for godly devotion! [11]

So the expectation of persecution, which is a fear as long as it is anticipated and no fun if it happens, is instilled into all JWs and impressed upon non-JWs who have studied Witness literature for only a few months. The book *The Truth That Leads To Eternal Life* was claimed by the Society to be listed third in the world's ten best-selling books, with 74 million copies printed. It was designed to be studied by interested people over a six month period. The last chapter tells these newly interested students:

'Circumstances may arise that threaten to interfere with your regular study of the Bible or your association with fellow Christians at congregational meetings. Opposition may cause the preaching work to become difficult, even dangerous' (p. 189).

That book has now been replaced with *You Can Live Forever In Paradise On Earth*, but the same persecution complex remains:

'What if your marriage mate has refused to study God's Word with you, or even opposes your Christian activity... It takes courage to do this work. Satan and his world are sure to try to stop you...' (pp. 248 and 253).

It is hardly surprising that JWs are not, in the main, cheerful people. Their persecution complex, combined with a negative anticipation of world events and a wearisome wait for the fearful 'great tribulation' prior to Armageddon, adds up to a lot of gloom. They do not have a lot to be happy about. Even though they are reasonably confident they are doing all the right things to survive Armageddon, they have recently been told that they will not know until the 'great tribulation' breaks out whether Jesus will put them as sheep to his right or as goats to his left side. So they concentrate their thoughts on a future paradise existence on earth to keep their spirits up. But with the Watch Tower Society's recent emphasis on the horrors of the coming 'great tribulation', they are not even being allowed much of that little luxury.

No miracles today

JWs are afraid of the miraculous, believing that the gifts of the Holy Spirit, speaking in tongues, healing, prophesying, interpretation of tongues etc, were expressly for the purpose of establishing the new Christian Church and that these gifts passed away after the death of the apostles. They also believe that any miracles done thereafter must be a counterfeit of the devil.[12] Indeed, they would take it as proof that the person performing such a miracle, even in the name of Christ, was *not* a Christian. 'Jesus said, "Not everyone who says to me, 'Lord, Lord,' will enter the kingdom of heaven, but only he who does the will of my Father who is in heaven. Many will say to me on that day, 'Lord, Lord, did we not prophesy in your name, and in your name drive out demons and perform many miracles?' Then I will tell them plainly, 'I never knew you. Away from me, you evildoers!'" (Matt. 7:21-23). But an examination of that passage indicates just the opposite. Jesus saying, 'Not everyone who says to me, "Lord, Lord," will enter the kingdom of heaven' implies that *some* who say, 'Lord, Lord,' *will* enter the kingdom of heaven. Otherwise, Jesus would have said, '*No-one* who says...' Many who claim to have performed miracles in the name of Christ will be exposed as false. But not all! Some will truly perform miracles in Jesus' name.

There can be no counterfeit without the genuine article. If there is no genuine article, there is either no counterfeit, or *everything* is counterfeit. Only by putting the genuine article alongside the counterfeit will the counterfeit be exposed. On the Day of

Judgment, those who truly called upon the Lord and performed miracles in his name will be identified as genuine, while imposters will be cast aside as evildoers. Performing miracles in the name of Jesus holds no fears for those who do so according to the will of the Father.

Of course, there is nothing wrong with attributing to the devil a work which is his. The JWs speak out strongly, for instance, against supposed 'faith healing', viewing it as either psychological or demonic. But because they do not distinguish between supposed faith healing and *divine* healing, they throw the baby out with the bath-water as the following quotation illustrates:

> 'It is noteworthy that during [faith healing] services people may "speak in tongues" or be "slain in the spirit".... Interestingly, such things are not unlike the fits and trances that involve those other religious healers, the voodoo priests and witch doctors... could it be that today's healers are in contact with a different source of power? [i.e. not from God.] This is very likely.... Modern faith healing, with its occult connections, is inevitably different from the healings performed by Jesus Christ.... This point about a different source of power becomes clearer when we realize that there is no reason to expect that the same kind of healing Jesus did would be practised today' (*Watchtower*, 1st September 1981, pp 5-7, article 'Faith Healing – Does it do any harm?').

Perhaps one mitigating factor is that the majority of JWs have been deceived into thinking the Holy Spirit is a mere force or power like electricity. They call him 'it'. Scriptures which clearly depict the Holy Spirit's divine personality have been explained away, rationalised – by those who claim to have His indwelling.[13] And if those who determine doctrine about the Holy Spirit's indwelling are *not themselves* indwelt by him, error is bound to result.

Four more possible fears have been added to our list:

(d) fear of becoming 'contaminated' by the world (i.e. everything and everyone outside the Watch Tower Society)

(e) fear of persecution

(f) fear of not being unique

(g) fear of miraculous operations of the Holy Spirit

From a JW point of view this list of fears would be preposterous. He would not consider himself to be frightened of such things, but confident in the face of them. But their confidence comes about by *not* facing up to these matters. If they did, many would become truly troubled.

His avoidance of all things worldly is an escape from responsibility, an avoidance of reality. His persecution complex is manufactured because he *cannot* be persecuted for bearing the name of Jesus whose name he does not bear. His pride in being unique is utter folly, given the clearly un-unique status of the Society and his attitude to the miraculous betrays lack of reverence for God's Holy Spirit.

Having considered some of the perplexing attitudes which mould JWs thinking about Christianity we must now turn the spotlight on Christians. Could they be found guilty of having perplexing attitudes about JWs? Are they as misinformed about JWs as JWs are about them? If there is to be a crossing of the divide between JWs and Christians, Christians need to be totally honest in their answers.

Chapter 2

Us And Them

'Jehovah's Witnesses? Oh, they are the people who don't believe in medicine.' This typifies the misunderstanding many people have. Another common misunderstanding is, 'They don't believe in Jesus, do they?' There is similar confusion about Mormons. Indeed, many Christians cannot even distinguish between Mormons and JWs. One Christian man I know made me shudder when he said he threatened visiting JWs with the police if they did not get off his doorstep.

The pendulum of misunderstanding swings all the way from Christians who say JWs must not be spoken to, let alone invited into one's home, to others who express dismay at any criticism of them. I was amazed at the strength of feeling stirred up by an article I wrote about JWs some years ago for a Christian magazine. Several readers' letters were printed saying it was un-Christian to criticise and 'attack' others. Christians needed to put their own house in order before tut-tutting at others. Thankfully, others wrote agreeing with the urgent need for JWs to be rescued from deception. This demonstrates clearly how considerable the misconceptions are. It may also help to explain why JWs are gaining nearly 323,000 converts every year.

If a Christian makes a false statement about JW belief, the Witness will show up the misunderstanding and confidently proceed with his indoctrination, having made his critic feel rather foolish. For example, if you wrongly accuse a Witness of refusing medical treatment, he will laughingly say he has just had his gall bladder removed by surgery, give a list of the medication he is taking and suggest you have confused him with Christian Scientists. He will then launch into an apparently biblical presentation of a form of medical treatment JWs *do* refuse, blood transfusion. By the time he has finished, you will be wishing you had never donated blood at the blood-bank!

You may accuse him of not believing in Jesus Christ as being the Son of God. With a pained expression on his face, he will pull out of his briefcase a *Watchtower* magazine; on its cover will be emblazoned, 'Jesus Christ – The Son of God'. Or, he will open one of his books to a chapter entitled, 'God Comes to Mankind's Rescue', full of scriptures about the atoning sacrifice of Jesus, the Son of God. An *informed* Christian would know how to advise a JW of his errors regarding blood transfusions and his meaning of the term 'Son of God'. An uninformed or, worse, *mis*informed, Christian would not know where error lay, let alone be able to point it out.

As for Christians who believe JWs are also Christians, well, all I can say, with deep respect is, heaven help them. They are liable to take Watch Tower literature, have the Witnesses call back, and within six months of regular visiting be poisoned against the true church of Christ. I know of two young women who, their Christian friends say, became Christians but who have stopped going to their local church after studying with JWs. Even if Christians have contact with JWs yet remain faithful to the Body of Christ, great harm can result to their children. I know one lady whose mother accepted literature and referred to the Witness as 'a visiting angel'. Although the mother never became a Witness, the daughter was deeply impressed by these visits and the literature and she became a Witness in her early twenties.

Nobody is immune to JW indoctrination. The June 22nd 1987 *Awake!* magazine even reported a haemophiliac becoming a JW. Although he had previously received over 900 blood transfusions, he immediately stopped having them, deciding this would 'prove his integrity to Jehovah'. Ironically the Society now 'permits' haemophiliac treatment. Although it continues to warn against Witnesses storing their own blood, some 2,500 units of blood require to be stored for a single haemophiliac treatment (See *The Watchtower*, 15 June 1985, p 30, and *Awake!* 22 June 1982, p 25).

We can learn something important from this. Christians have good reason to hold JWs in healthy respect. Their method of proselytizing is powerfully effective, whether in the face of opposition or sympathy. It is no wonder that most Christians are anxious to dispatch JWs from their doorstep with as few words said as possible.

Are JWs Antichrist?
In fact, some Christians believe JWs fit the description of the antichrist and the deceiver detailed in 2 John 7-11:

'For many deceivers have gone out into the world who do not confess Jesus Christ as coming in the flesh. This is a deceiver and an antichrist. Look to yourselves, that we do not lose those things we worked for, but that we may receive a full reward. Whoever transgresses and does not abide in the doctrine of Christ does not have God. He who abides in the doctrine of Christ has both the Father and the Son. If anyone comes to you and does not bring this doctrine, do not receive him into your house nor greet him; for he who greets him shares in his evil deeds' (NKJV).

In this passage the identifying mark of a deceiver and an antichrist is his refusal to acknowledge that Jesus Christ is coming in the flesh. Other translations render verse seven as, '...who confess not that Jesus Christ is come in the flesh' (KJV), or similarly, putting the emphasis on Jesus' first coming, not his second, future coming. What do JWs teach about both Christ's first coming and his second coming?

With regard to Christ's first coming, JWs openly confess he came in the flesh: 'So Jesus was not an imaginary person. He really lived as a man on earth' (*You can live forever in Paradise on earth*, p. 57). They believe in his prehuman spiritual existence in heaven, that he was then conceived by the power of the Holy Spirit by the virgin Mary and born as a human baby. Truly man, he was put to death and he truly died. Now comes an area of difficulty. After his death, JWs maintain that God 'disposed' of Christ's human body.[1] He was resurrected as a spirit creature who materialised in various bodily forms to appear to his disciples. Because 1 Peter 3:18 says,

'...being put to death in the flesh but made alive by the Spirit,' they have had to render their NWT thus: '...he being put to death in the flesh, but being made alive *in* the spirit.'[2] (italics mine).

Despite having no scriptural grounds for saying Christ's material body no longer exists and that he now has a spirit form, JWs hold firmly to this notion and it colours their beliefs about his second appearance. 'Every eye will see him' becomes, in their interpretation, 'Every *spiritual* eye will see him.' Only those with 'eyes of understanding' observed his return which was supposed to have taken place invisibly in 1914.[3] Only JWs 'saw' this happen. Jesus' warning in Matthew 24:24-28 surely encompasses such false teaching.

JWs clearly do *not* believe in a visible, bodily second appearance of Christ. Is *this* what 2 John 7-11 warns against, or is it only speaking of Christ's first bodily coming? There are conflicting views on this. Some who understand New Testament [NT] Greek say the grammatical construction does not allow for a future application; it is only referring to Christ's *first* bodily appearance. Others say that the contrasting use of the present participle (cf. Revelation 1:8) allows for inclusion of belief with regard to Christ's second coming.

Perhaps the most pertinent comment on the matter is found in the *New International Commentary*. Those who deny Christ's first bodily appearance will naturally deny any such second bodily appearance. 'Both beliefs stand or fall together.' So, although the JWs believe in the first bodily appearance, they have still managed to fall at the second 'hurdle' of belief.

This being the case, and thus the JWs possibly fitting the description of those who have committed an 'evil deed' with regard to teaching about Christ, should we take literally the command not to receive them into our homes or to greet them?

First, it must be noted to whom this epistle was addressed. It was to 'the elect lady and her children' (see 1 Peter 5:13), taken to mean the church. It therefore seems that church fellowship is the issue. The welcome would refer to church approval or support. Second, it must also be noted that individual church members cannot do with impunity what is wrong for the church to do collectively. If it is wrong for the body of Christ to welcome, approve and support heretical teachers who try to infiltrate the church, then it is equally wrong for members of that body to encourage such teachers who try to infiltrate their household.

It seems to me that a wise Christian attitude would be to have a clear understanding of the dangerous nature of JW teaching. Such an awareness will prevent us from showing approval of their false teaching. This awareness of the error of Society teaching, however, will not prevent us from reaching out to individual Witnesses with the truth once we have established whether such an individual is the deceiver or the deceived.

The people on your doorstep presenting JW false doctrine are not the *originators* of the heresy. Only a tiny core of individuals have ever been responsible for JW false teaching. And even from this tiny percentage, at least one has a strong Christian testimony. He is Raymond Franz, who served for nine years on the Governing Body of the Society, and maintains he was a Christian at that time although he had to leave the Society and is now disfellowshiped from it. The teaching about Christ's invisible, spiritual, second coming was in place before he became a member of this Governing Body.

Thousands of JWs leave the movement every year, many becoming Christians. As the process of leaving takes, on average, two years, with the doubting JW often continuing his activity to the last, who knows but that the next Witness on your doorstep is already in the throes of re-evaluating his beliefs? My own conversion was the direct result of a Christian lady twice inviting me into her home and then praying for me for two years. Did God bless disobedience to his commands? Did he honour the prayers of someone who had flouted his word? I think not.

It has to be acknowledged also that John said these antichrists do not *continue* (or abide) in the teaching of Christ. This suggests that, at one time, they had the teaching of Christ but then abandoned it. Most JWs have never had the teaching of Christ. They have either had JW indoctrination from birth, as in my case, or a nominal Christian upbringing, which is not truly Christian at all. A good number have had no contact with Christianity in any guise whatever.

If a Witness had professed Christ to be his Saviour and then renounced such belief in preference for JW teaching, perhaps he may be such a one as is described in 2 John verse 9. A couple of direct questions at the outset should satisfy a concerned Christian whether the JW talking to him comes into that category or not. But you are far more likely to find the deceived on your doorstep, and not the deceiver.

A better response?

Assuming, then, that the injunction of 2 John 7-11 does not apply, how should we react? Because of the difficulty and frustration involved in successfully engaging with JWs, it would indeed be wise to exercise prayerful caution with them. Sadly, few Christians get that far, simply panicking when surprised by a JW visit, blurting a feeble excuse and shutting the door. And the next time they see uninvited 'guests' walk up the garden path, they may pretend they are not at home rather than go through the same discomfort. Most Christians show every evidence of being frightened of JWs.

What is the situation with non-Christians? To be honest, it is usually incredibly hard to spot *any* difference, unless bad language is employed by the householder. But non-Christians are inclined to react just as badly as Christians and, again, fear is the predominant force. So often the same weak excuses are given or the same inadequate objections offered. Having spent over fourteen years actively involved in JW ministry, I can say that the number of people who responded in a Christ-like way to me could be counted on two hands.

What is a Christ-like attitude? Reflect for a moment on Christ's attitude to sinners. He listened to them even though he knew they were sinners, asking them thought-provoking questions to stimulate their interest. And he did not condemn them. Compare his attitude to that of the Pharisees when they questioned the man born blind whom Jesus healed (John 9:1-34). They took offence and accused him of being a sinner, although they were sinners themselves, and threw him out in a rage! When JWs call at our homes, do we reflect the manner of Christ or the manner of the Pharisees?

In my experience, those few Christ-like individuals I met are vivid in my memory. Their response always took me by surprise. First and foremost they listened respectfully to what I'd come to say. Then they said something that stopped me in my tracks. Some produced their Bibles and quoted from them. Others raised scriptural objections or questions. They did what so few people managed to do, they made me stop and *think*.

Sometimes return visits continued the discussion. Other times the encounter only lasted a few minutes on the doorstep. But I was filled with a grudging admiration that here were people who knew what they believed and why. What is more, they were prepared to share their faith with me. Of course, I did not even consider the possibility that they were right and I now realise that most of what they said did not register with me. Yet that did not matter. What mattered to me was the demonstration of a sincere, caring attitude. *That* registered. Those people were concerned that I might not be right before God. They wanted to help me. Even though I 'knew' it was *they* who were not right before God, I was touched by... well, *something* about them. I now know what that 'something' was. It was the Spirit of Christ. I did not know that after my departure from their doorstep those Christians were fervently praying for my salvation. If I had known, I would have been even more touched.

I reckon that I must have knocked on the doors of some 38,000 homes in my fourteen active years as a JW. To say that only a handful of individuals demonstrated a noticeably Christ-like attitude is appalling. Had more Christians displayed Christ's love to me, might I have been helped out of the Watch Tower Society much sooner?

JW door-knocking (1,144,566,849 hours of it world wide in 1999) serves as a wonderful reinforcement of JW prejudice against the Church. So few seem to demonstrate the Spirit of Christ. We know that not everyone who professes to be a Christian is a Christian, but JWs do not make that differentiation. Anyone who says he is a Christian is taken as an example of what the churches are producing. Much of that apparent 'produce' is totally God-dishonouring. Others can only be described as hopelessly apathetic. When compared to the zealous, sincere, law-abiding, morally upright type of individual 'produced' by the Watch Tower Society, who can blame Witnesses for feeling repelled at what, to them, is the hypocrisy of Christendom? Indeed, some of the worst responses to JWs come from the clergy! Generally speaking, they fall into two classes. They are either disdainfully haughty or apologetically nervous. Either way, the clergy's doors are rarely long in closing. But I thank God for those few clergymen who patiently responded to my doorstep butterfly sermons, especially the one who startled me into re-examining my beliefs with the simple warning, 'JWs are a dangerous sect.'

Now that I've left the Watch Tower Society, I can appreciate why JWs get the negative, brusque responses they do. Many of them ask for it by being pushy, argumentative and inconsiderate. One reader of the UK newspaper, *The Daily Mail*, wrote in to the letters column protesting at the plague of JWs on his housing estate. 'Why can't they take "No" for an answer and stop trying to sell religion on the doorstep? Even a high-pressure salesman knows when to give up!' (21 June 1988)

Even those who are courteous, tactful and pleasant still frighten people off with their wizardry in turning to proof texts and their immediate answers to objections. Feelings of frustration, inadequacy and dismay are to be expected from unprepared householders. But I still understand the JW point of view: 'If we can learn to handle the Bible and speak out in public about our beliefs, why can't churchgoers? Surely this is just one more evidence that God's holy spirit is blessing the Watch Tower Society – that God is using *us* to spread the good news. The laity don't even know what this good news of the kingdom is, poor souls. It's not their fault because the clergymen themselves don't seem to believe the good news, nor are they preaching it to their people.'

This is what I mean by JW door-knocking experiences reinforcing their anti-Church prejudice. Until Christians start using God's word, the Bible, to enable them to 'speak the truth in love' to JWs, those prejudices will continue to be confirmed instead of refuted. But if Christians respond to the challenge of JWs we might begin to see them converted to

Christianity instead of being drawn further into the JW fold.

Does the task sound too daunting, or too difficult for you? Then consider my experience. See how God raised up various individuals, at opportune times, to turn me from an attacker of the Body of Christ into one of its members. Take heart from the role played by prayer, from start to finish. See how God dealt with my fear. Notice how love was the antidote. After reading this experience your fear will surely start to be replaced with love – love for the deceived JWs and love for God whose mercy encompasses them as much as it does you. Read on, and catch the vision!

Chapter 3

A Journey into Fear

Fear can have complex causes, but frequently one element is anticipated pain or punishment. The prospect of suffering physical pain may cause a reaction of shrinking back; mental pain can result in withdrawing into one's self; fear of punishment (even though not deserved) can spur people on to defensive action, or to obey those who threaten the punishment in order to avoid or minimise it. This kind of fear has, for centuries, been used manipulatively by those who would wield power over others.

The fear employed by the Watch Tower Society is never overt. Whenever the Society mentions punishment issues, like the death and destruction of Armageddon or the possibility of being disfellowshiped, it always appeals to the Bible as its source and places the onus for avoiding punishment on each individual's shoulders. The Society is careful to foster an image of a caring 'mother' who acts and speaks lovingly to keep Witnesses on the straight and narrow, for their own good. For people like myself, brought up by zealous JW parents, it was virtually impossible to see the Society in anything other than a benign light. It wasn't until I attempted to leave that I discovered how subtly fear was used as a controlling device.

In my childhood years there were very few occasions of punishment or fear. When I was about seven or eight one of my older brothers asked me to run away with him. This was on a Tuesday night when some of the local JWs met at our house for what was called 'the group study'. My brother had run away several times before. Of the five of us, he experienced the greatest torment at being brought up the JW way. I agreed to accompany him and off we set, walking from Kirkcaldy along the coastal road. By the time we arrived at East Wemyss it was dark. Then, for no reason that was apparent to me, he suddenly decided to call at a house to ask for money for the bus fare home. We waited for a bus, the money having been given to us, and returned home. Afraid of the angry reception awaiting us, I would much sooner have continued walking! That was a rare occasion when I was smacked and I knew it was for having done wrong. I did not do it again, although my brother did.

Only recently have I learned from my brother something of the manipulative fear and punishment inflicted upon him from early childhood, leading to his elopement while I was still at school. To this day he recalls with cool anger the memories of protracted beatings, prefaced by lengthy discourses, all designed to intimidate and subjugate a boy who, in his father's eyes, was in need of discipline. In truth, he was in need of love.

For myself the most disturbing feelings of fear came at school, as a result of our JW upbringing. At primary school, when morning assembly was unapologetically based on the Christian faith, my twin sister, Lesley, and I were forbidden to attend. Our JW parents heeded Watch Tower Society 'advice' to keep us from such religious 'contamination'. Yet it troubled us, being made to stand apart from everyone else, conspicuous by our absence. We devised a compromise, just between the two of us. There was nothing wrong with being in the school choir, that was not forbidden, so we joined it and attended assembly as choir members! The guilty fact of singing hymns was never mentioned to our parents. We knew they would disapprove.

Christmas and birthday celebrations were also forbidden. One winter afternoon, as Lesley and I walked home from primary school, we lingered at a brightly lit shop window in Commercial Street, mesmerised by a very small plastic Christmas tree with gaudy baubles hanging from its branches. This tiny object so appealed to us, we pooled our pocket money and bought it. At home, in our room, we placed the sparkling little object of our fascination on a table, and knelt down to sing in a whisper, 'Silent Night'. We didn't want to be discovered, but the primary feeling was not so much fear as loss at missing out on something rather wonderful. So we had our own private little bit of Christmas heedless of the parental disapproval that it might invoke.

However, our parents heartily approved when, aged twelve, Lesley and I asked to be baptised as JWs. We had responded to one of many talks at the Kingdom Hall about the imperative need to dedicate ourselves to Jehovah before Armageddon, and to symbolise this by submitting to total water immersion. That two twelve year olds should make such a request unprompted illustrates how much effect years of attendance at meetings can have. It is difficult for outsiders to appreciate the measure of mind control these exert.

A typical midweek evening meeting followed this programme:

Theocratic School
Song and Welcome.

Item 1: 15 minute talk on 'Share joyfully with Jesus Christ in Jehovah's work', a five page article from an issue of *The Watchtower*. This 'Instruction Talk' is given preferably by an elder.

Item 2: Psalm 72:1-20. A five minute presentation by the Ministry School Overseer, or another qualified elder assigned by him, giving highlights of the passage and asking questions on it.

Item 3: *Bible Topics for Discussion* booklet No 47B, 'How can the true religion be identified?' A six minute talk assigned to two sisters. A variety of settings can be adopted for this, e.g., a situation at home, in the field service or in the congregation.

Item 4: *Holy Spirit* book p. 166 para 7 to p. 168 para 11. A six minute demonstration of a Bible study taken by a sister with another sister acting as an interested householder. The printed instructions read, 'This assignment in the school should encourage those who are not yet conducting home Bible studies to work toward this end and help publishers who do conduct them to improve.... If an answer [to a printed question in the book] is incomplete, the conductor should ask auxiliary questions.'

Item 5: A six minute talk given by a brother with some experience to the entire audience based on two pages from *Awake!*

After items 2, 3, 4 and 5 the School overseer would highlight important points the students might not have emphasised sufficiently. While I was a JW, counsel on speaking skills was given publicly, immediately after each talk. It is now given privately afterwards.

That Ministry School took an hour. It was followed by The Service Meeting based on another internal leaflet which is printed monthly by the Society. It went like this:

Service Meeting
Song 73 followed by a fifteen minute question and answer 'discussion' of an article in this internal leaflet entitled 'Showing we care about our young people'. The article contained such advice as, 'How fine it would be for the elders to include one or two of them among those whom they converse with when at the meetings.... Concern for young people is shown by working with them in the field service on a regular basis. Their help can be enlisted in doing work necessary to maintain the Kingdom Hall.... There are young men and women who are doing quite well, progressing nicely, and are in a fine position to assist other young people in the congregation.... Perhaps you could invite them to accompany you in field service.'

Then came a twelve minute 'discussion'-cum-talk given by 'an elder who has a good rapport with young people'. If no such elder existed one who was not gifted in that area would be used instead. The internal leaflet said, 'Have a discussion showing an elder talking with a young brother right after weekly

Theocratic School and Service Meeting. Elder discusses with young brother his Bible reading for that week. He encourages him to make fine progress. During the conversation he asks about his school studies and activities and if there are any particular problems in school. Elder takes the time to share practical suggestions and to encourage the brother. He leaves by making arrangements to work with him in field service that week-end.'[1]

That sketch was followed by an eighteen minute mini-*Watchtower* study from an article entitled 'Youths – are you on the road to real success?' A youth would read the 'important' passages. And the meeting ended with a seven minute slot for a song and prayer, immediately after which the few young people present slipped out to avoid any enthused elder trying to practice such exhortations on them!

Both of the hour long meetings were starchy as no theatricals were allowed. We thanked God silently for the rare moments of laughter injected, sometimes unwittingly, by the more extrovert individuals on the platform. Before writing the above account I asked my husband, Derek, how he would describe JW meetings. Without a moment's hesitation he answered, 'Unremitting boredom.' Perhaps I should have warned you!

Despite such patronising and unspontaneous tactics Lesley and I, by the time we were twelve, asked to be baptised. After being questioned on our supposed dedication to Jehovah by Fred Scott, a lovely elderly man who took the bread and wine at the Memorial, arrangements were made for our baptism. This ceremony was carried out at a big

56

international assembly of JWs at Twickenham, London. I recall the preceding hour's lecture majored on *not* believing in the Trinity, even though we were to be baptised in the name (singular) of the Father, the Son and the Holy Spirit.

Our baptism did not lessen the continued discomfort we felt at secondary school with such things as singing the national anthem. This, too, was wrong according to the Watch Tower Society. We had to tell teachers that we would not stand up or sing the anthem. A great furore occurred when we said we could not stand on the stage with the rest of the pupils performing *H.M.S. Pinafore* to sing the anthem. Lesley and I felt miserable. We hated all this controversy. On the evening of the performance we ended up slipping in at the wings to join the back row, our diminutive stature ensuring that our parents would not see us. They remained seated in the audience. When our class went to the Adam Smith Hall to see a professional production of *The Mikado*, we were ushered out into a corridor by an understanding music teacher just before the end, thus saving us the embarrassment of remaining seated at that dreaded drum roll heralding the anthem.

An interesting detail about negative Society influence regarding music was shown by our parents' attitude to Lesley and I having piano lessons. They encouraged us and we enjoyed learning, but it was not until some years after my lessons stopped that I discovered how my parents had effectively tied my music teacher's hands behind his back. At the outset they showed him the little *Kingdom Songs* music book then used at all JW meetings and said words to the effect, 'We simply want the girls to be able to play this music for our meetings so don't put them through any exams or grades. Just teach them to play this.' So, for about seven years, we were taught to sight-read *without* being taught music theory! We never had scales, or arpeggios, or exams. No wonder we enjoyed lessons! Perhaps that is how we attained a moderate degree of sight-reading; practice was hardly irksome. It was, however, extremely slow progress and now I realise what a wasted opportunity it was.

When we came to the stage of wanting to go dancing and permission was refused, we resorted to lying, saying we were going to the cinema when, in fact, we went to the dance hall. What a pity our parents did not replace their negative attitude to dancing with a positive alternative. Needless to say, our early teenage years were not too happy as we walked a tightrope between satisfying our parents with their JW rules and dealing with our craving to be accepted by our peer group. We fell between two stools, knowing we were doing wrong and that we would be punished should our deceptions be discovered.

However, the persistent pressure of JW indoctrination combined with our strong feelings of guilt paid dividends. Lesley and I gradually came around to JW thinking and decided to launch ourselves wholeheartedly into Witness activity. In our mid teens we started 'pioneering', much to our parents' delight. This involved subsisting on a part-time job whilst devoting one hundred hours each month to door-knocking – 'the work'. We became more and more convinced that this was the right thing to do. Armageddon, God's battle to destroy all wickedness, was imminent. People *had* to be warned. No-one but JWs were sounding the alarm. If people did not believe this warning and become JWs, they would die at Armageddon, never to be resurrected. We felt little fear at the prospect of Armageddon because we were confident we would survive it. After all, we were dedicated, baptised JWs, now totally devoted to the witness work and we attended all the meetings. We had nothing to fear now. Our days of rebellion and disobedience were over. What relief we felt!

Lesley married a JW pioneer and they moved to England. I progressed to the rank of Special Pioneer. The Watch Tower Society invited me to join this esteemed core of financially supported Witnesses who devoted one hundred and fifty hours monthly to the work. Our income from the Society was less than the state pension, but with my Special Pioneer partner and another Regular Pioneer girl sharing a rundown room and kitchen in Saltcoats, we struggled by. A good sense of humour and a disregard for the finer things in life made our task acceptable, even quite enjoyable. I had no regrets whatever. Being totally convinced the Society was right in every regard I felt honoured to be part of its Special Pioneer ranks.

Those Special Pioneering days ended when I married Derek, a Regular Pioneer who had given up his job in Sheffield to come to Scotland for this work. I continued Regular Pioneering until pregnancy made its particular demands on me. From then onwards I was a good 'publisher', trying to spend ten hours each month on the work, though this was not often achieved after the birth of our first son. Still, we went to all the meetings, taking the baby, despite there being no creche facilities during the two-hour long, twice weekly, meetings. Every weekend we went on the work, baby being wheeled around in his pram as I had been by my parents.

Some post-natal depression did not deter me from having another child. Indeed, the strangest thing happened just after I'd sold the first baby's pram and cot; for the first time in my life I was swamped with overwhelming maternal urges to have another baby. I had never experienced even the slightest maternal instincts prior to this. A few months later, when pregnancy was confirmed, those foreign feelings vanished, never to return again. With hindsight I can see the hand of divine providence in this, but at that time I was unaware that this second pregnancy was to result in five of the darkest, most depressing years of my life.

The depression years
The spasmodic bouts of depression experienced previously became much more frequent after our second son was born. Their severity was such that it seemed as if every particle of joy I had ever known was gone for ever, never to return. In my condition, the children seemed to be the cause of my misery and I could find no pleasure or comfort in them. Days were successions of screaming bouts followed by grim silences, and nights were frequently sleepless and saturated in tears. There was no-one I could confide in, especially as a *Watchtower* article on the

subject of depression implied that the problem largely lay in thinking too much about one's self. So I continued staunchly with the door-to-door work and Witness activity. It did not help, only serving to make me more exhausted.

Many times I felt I would rather be dead than have to go through another bout of depression. My outbursts of temper became so bad I would suffer palpitations and my right hand would lock in a clenched position. I was so severe with the children when angered that I sometimes shook them violently as I screamed at them. Feeling dangerously close to the brink of insanity, I went to my GP, but the tranquillisers he prescribed doped me so much I knew I would be unable to drive whilst taking them. As we lived in the country and the car was my lifeline, I threw the pills away and didn't bother going back. Four more nightmare years dragged by.

One night, after lying exhausted in bed, unable to sleep and sobbing into the pillow, I went through to the living room to sit by the fire's dying embers, heartbroken and despairing. Choking back the tears, I cried out feebly, 'Jehovah, help me... help me.' The last few faltering flames flickered out and the darkness seemed to shut me in. There was no reply.

The discovery years

Grimly, I continued doing the only thing I knew I could, and should do, which was going on the work. It was at this time that I knocked on the door of a large house one Saturday morning in June 1977 and, after that, life was never quite the same. The young man who politely listened to me surprised me by saying he was a clergyman. I was surprised, not that he was a clergyman, but that such a person would listen to me politely. Normally, clergymen treated me either with scornful disdain or embarrassed discomfort. But Mr. MacKay did neither. After listening he said, 'But, with respect, don't you think....' and so the conversation developed. What we talked about I can no longer recall. It ended after about half an hour in stalemate. As I made to go, Mr. MacKay's parting remark was, 'Jehovah's Witnesses are a dangerous sect.' This outrageous comment shocked me deeply. He had not said it with malice or irritation. Quite the opposite – he had spoken gently. But I was shocked.

How could JWs be called dangerous? A more peaceable, law-abiding, decent group of people would be impossible to find! Puzzled, I could not dismiss this challenge and determined to resolve it. So I went to the local library to sniff around the theology section, looking for any comments about this alleged 'dangerous' nature of JWs. I came away with some respected works by renowned clerics.

Just at that time, as I worked another area, I came across a lady who was to have a much greater impact on me but, this time, without my realising it. Mrs. Hodgson also listened respectfully to me. Then she invited me into her home. We soon began to express our differing views on the person of Christ. Mrs. Hodgson insisted that her Bible said Jesus was God. I 'knew' that the correct translation said he was merely 'a god'. She agreed to have me call back the following week to continue the discussion. I prepared thoroughly for that return visit, confident that I could show her the error of her beliefs.[2]

The return visit did not go as I had hoped. I can remember as I sat on Mrs. Hodgson's settee, the tears welling up because I realised she would not be moved. She was such a lovely lady, I could not bear to think of her dying at Armageddon because she believed the Trinity doctrine. Yet I could not dissuade her. The call ended. There was no point in my trying to keep the contact going. She was quietly resolute.

Very quickly she faded from my memory. I had much more urgent matters to concentrate on. Suddenly I found myself swamped with information which was alarming, to say the least. One of the books I obtained from the library was all about JWs, from the point of view of one who had been brought up by JW parents. But the author, Alan Rogerson, had done his homework. He had researched the Society's archives, listing a catalogue of false prophecies and changed beliefs. Horrified, I checked out all his references.

His allegations were well founded. Now I was beginning to understand why JWs could be considered dangerous. Those in command of the organisation appeared to have conducted a cover-up over the years, manipulating millions of people into obeying their every word as God's gospel truth. It could have been done because they were too frightened to admit to the errors clearly displayed in their own literature. But the reason many of those changes were not noticed by the membership was that new editions of the publications were slightly amended.

A vitally important doctrinal change had been effected by altering one little word. As late on as 1916 the Society was still maintaining that Christ's second presence occurred in the year 1874. (See 1916 editions of *Studies in the Scriptures* Vol. 4, pp. 612, 616 and 621.) The 1907 edition of *Thy Kingdom Come* said, '...and the full establishment of the Kingdom of God in the earth *at* 1914.' However, the 1927 edition of that book said, '...and the full establishment of the Kingdom of God in the earth *after* 1914.' (Emphasis mine.) Post 1914 events could not be made to support the belief that Christ had come in 1874 and that Armageddon would be over and done with by 1914. So, instead of 1914 being the *end* of 'the time of the end', it became the *start* of 'the time of the end'!

The Witnesses have always maintained that the start of this time period is marked by Christ's *invisible* presence. They also try to give the impression that their beliefs about 1914 have never changed. This simply is not true. But post-1917 JWs would have to spot such changes in the appropriate editions of those old books to know that. Being brought up as a JW some forty years after this doctrinal change, I had no idea that Christ's second presence was said to have occurred in 1874 and that Armageddon was prophesied as due to end in 1914. The Society had devoted its literature to emphasising how free from doctrinal change it had been!

It is no wonder that the Society is frightened to admit its errors because when those particular errors were realised in the 1920s, thousands of Witnesses left. Rogerson showed that since then many more false prophecies and beliefs have been proclaimed. If they, too, were exposed, another mass exodus would result. I began to realise that I would most likely become one of the disenchanted leavers.

The correspondence years

I began an anxious correspondence with the Society about this unwelcome information. Their replies were *not* reassuring and my doubts remained. Perplexed, I checked out other aspects of Witness beliefs, particularly the denial of the Trinity and the still current, but perhaps for not much longer, view that Christ's second presence took place in 1914.

At this time I met another clergyman who also seemed prepared to talk to me, but he kept breaking our appointments. It was unfortunate, particularly as my JW mother-in-law got to know of it. She lived next door to us, and the clergyman telephoned her number by mistake when cancelling one appointment. She confronted me with the call, wanting to know who had an appointment with this clergyman. She thought it was an evening appointment, which enabled me to deny it as our meeting had been for the morning. But this less-than-forthright answer was caused by fear. I knew I was not seeing this clergyman as a JW out to convert him. I realised *I* was the one who could end up being converted! I was frightened, and I ended up doing what I was dismayed at the Society for doing – stating what was strictly true, but omitting other facts which would have given a more honest answer.

The next time I visited the clergyman he had forgotten about our arrangement and he was on the verge of going out. My nerve failed me at that point. What had possessed me, going to the clergy of

Christendom for help? I should unburden myself to those in Jehovah's organisation who were looking after his sheep. Frightened at how far I had gone, I turned to one JW elder who, I knew, would give me a sympathetic hearing.

To my relief, Dick seemed to understand and he set about allaying my fears. His explanations seemed plausible. Yes, the Society *had* made some mistakes, but God continued guiding and correcting them, letting the light of his truth grow ever brighter as Armageddon approached. Even if they had been wrong, on occasion, where else could this truth be found? None of the churches believed those fundamental doctrines which God had revealed to his people – doctrines like Christ coming in 1914, a paradise earth in store for the obedient, preaching this good news to all the nations, and so on. Where else could anyone go to find God's blessing? What other people were so united in love and devotion to each other and to God but JWs? I soaked up his assurances, feeling relieved at having drawn back from the brink of a dangerous cliff edge.

The relief did not last long. A *Watchtower* magazine (1st March 1979) was published with an article entitled, 'Put Faith in Jehovah's Victorious Organization'. It gave a glowing resumé of the Society's history. The whitewash was sickening. The Society did not admit to such cardinal errors as Christ's second presence having occurred in 1874; to Armageddon being predicted for 1914, then 1915, then 1925; to Russell, in his person, being hailed as 'the faithful and wise servant'; to Babylon the Great having fallen prior to 1914.

What sickened me most was the realisation that if I had not researched so fully, I would have believed that article, repeating portions like a parrot in answer to the printed questions for each paragraph at the Sunday morning *Watchtower* study.

Because I just could not go to that meeting without commenting on what had been omitted in the article I stayed at home. This deliberate avoidance of meetings was a serious matter for me. I had never done it before. I had never feigned illness, nor planned outings to coincide with meeting times, just to miss meetings. They were crucially important. Now I was starting to miss more and more. So was Derek. He was disturbed at the adverse effect late nights were having on our eldest son's schooling. The child was liable to fall asleep at his desk on Wednesday and Friday mornings. So we took it in turns to stay home on meeting nights, to put the children to bed. Somehow, he seemed to have far more turns than me!

I discovered later that Derek had long been disenchanted with several aspects of the Society, not least their recent elder arrangement. After years of proudly boasting that JWs had no clergy/laity structure, they introduced an elder system which was just that. Only elders could give public talks and have positions of authority and leadership in the congregations. Happily, this and other things led to Derek leaving at around the same time as I did, otherwise we could have ended with a ruined marriage. He had supported me faithfully through all my times of depression, yet had he remained a loyal JW and I had left, he would likely have abandoned me. And *vice versa*. Such is the immense pressure couples come under when one partner leaves the Society.

Taking the place of Christ

The next article in that *Watchtower* magazine was equally nauseating. It was called, 'To Whom Shall We Go But Jesus Christ?' It was designed to prove Christ's continual presence with his followers, not only through the holy spirit, but also through his 'faithful and discreet slave' class. Proof of going to Jesus was to go to this slave. No-one could go to Jesus *without* first going to the faithful and discreet slave (paragraph 15)! The catalogue of errors made by this slave class was dismissed in the space of six sentences as merely an opportunity for the rank and file to show loyalty and love to the slave class, whose motives were sound, even if their pronouncements were not. No list of unsound pronouncements followed, however. Why not, I wondered, if the slave class felt so sure of their followers' loyalty and love?[3]

The article concluded, 'To stay with Jesus Christ is to stay with those whom he is pleased to use. Outside the true Christian congregation [JWs] what alternative organization is there?' A bewildered scribble I made at the time said, 'Who needs an organisation if one has Christ? I thought this article was about going to Jesus Christ!' Nowhere in either of those two articles was anyone advised to *first* go to Jesus Christ before expecting to learn who comprised the faithful and discreet slave. By the time I reached the end of that *Watchtower*, my credibility had reached saturation point.

My reading of library books became prolific. I tackled major works on the Trinity, realising the extent of the cover-up job the Society had done on this subject. I was not yet persuaded that this doctrine was scriptural, but I was horrified at the methods the Society had employed to discredit the teaching. The Society quoted Greek scholars out of context and mistranslated the Bible in their *New World Translation*,[4] adding words here, changing words there, and omitting words elsewhere.[5]

That July 1st *Watchtower* contained a typical example of quoting out of context in order to make the person quoted appear to support Society teaching, when he did not. German Doctor of Theology, J. Schneider, was partially quoted on the subject of God and Christ. The Society quoted him in order to prove that: '...when theologians confine themselves to what the Bible, rather than later Church doctrines says, often the result is what this magazine has long been championing.' I obtained the book from which Dr. Schneider was partially quoted and soon realised the danger of accepting, without verification, the Society's arguments and conclusions.

In complete opposition to what *The Watchtower* has long been championing, Dr. Schneider supported the RSV translation of John 1:1 which contradicts the Society's translation. Dr. Schneider said:

'The fact that there is no definite article before *theos* here has been taken to imply that the Word may be understood as being some kind of divine being but not in the fullest sense of the term. Such views have been put forward from Origen whose views were

69

taken up by the Arians in the fourth century, to the Jehovah's Witnesses today.'

He concluded his article by saying:

'E Stauffer is doubtless correct when he writes, "The Christology of the N.T. is carried to its logical conclusion with the thorough-going designation of Christ as *theos*."' – God!

A few pages later Dr. Schneider wrote another article under the heading '8. The Trinity.' He made the point that the New Testament does not contain the *developed* doctrine of the Trinity, but showed, briefly, the basis for the doctrine. As the article was only of three paragraph's duration, many other theological books were referred to for further information on the subject.[6]

After reading Dr. Schneider's articles, I came to the conclusion that because he referred to the Witnesses as supporters of Arius, the Society had decided to refer to him as a supporter of *The Watchtower*! Nothing could be further from the truth.

Vital alterations
NWT additions, omissions and alterations to the Bible deserve a book to themselves. Adding the words 'union with' where scripture only has 'in' denies the truth that Christ dwells in the believer by the Holy Spirit. Omitting the word 'me' in John 14:14 denies the believer the right to pray to Jesus.[7] Taking the Greek word *kolasis* and rendering it 'cutting off' detracts severely from the real meaning of

punishment (Mat 25:46). Adding the word 'other' in Colossians 1:16, 17 implies that Christ is a created being instead of the Creator. Changing Revelation 3:14 to read that Christ is '...the beginning of the creation by God' does likewise.

It was dawning on me that 'proving' the Trinity one way or the other was not the only important matter. It was just as urgent to establish the integrity and scholastic honesty of the opposing parties. On this issue the Society's case fell apart at the seams. Yet they had the cheek to accuse Christian clergy of distorting God's truth!

I felt a pressing need to give the much maligned and misrepresented clergy a chance to speak for themselves. I had only ever listened to the Watch Tower Society. Now I would give 'the opposition' a hearing. It was time to start going to church. But to let you understand something of the significance of a JW going in to a church service for the very first time, I will describe in detail what my first church service was like.

Crossing the line
Deciding to go to Mr. MacKay's church one sunny, mild spring Sunday morning, I arrived in good time, but not in good spirits. The physical act of walking up those steps in broad daylight and going into a church with a crowd of people overwhelmed me with fear and guilt. For what seemed like eternity I stood in the vestibule, torn between sitting down in a pew or running out. I was afraid my visit to church might come to the attention of fellow Witnesses. What had possessed me, going to *this* church, most of whose

members' homes I would have called at as a Witness? What possible explanation could I give for me – a Jehovah's Witness – attending a service of 'Babylon the Great'? Could I explain it by stressing that I was attending but not participating; I was there purely as an observer? Maybe that would wash with the Witnesses, but what about God? What if Christendom *was* a 'harlot' in God's eyes? What view would he take of me? At any moment I expected fire to come down from heaven to strike me dead.

But the minister came in, the service started, and I slipped in at the back. I was so overwhelmed with fear, guilt and unfamiliarity with procedure, I could not remember anything of the sermon. The whole thing struck me as a stand-up-sit-down-keep-moving routine. I did not know if I was coming or going, and then the collection plate came round. I passed it on, none the heavier. Only one phrase in the service stuck with me. After reading a Bible passage, the minister said, 'And God will bless the public reading of his word.' I felt annoyed when he said that, for it struck me as merely a reading, with no explanation. It did not dawn on me till much later that the sermon which followed was to be an exposition of that passage. The final hymn was sung (not by me), the benediction given, and people started to file out.

At that point I realised I had overlooked something. At the Kingdom Hall people mill around for half an hour chatting, but here everyone left straight away, shaking hands with the minister at the door. I had planned on having a word with Mr. MacKay, but that would be impossible unless I stood behind, waiting until everyone had gone. My knees were still knocking and when it came to it, I just did not have the nerve. Instead I hurried home to write in my diary, 'I went. I really did! And it was the most nerve-racking experience. I won't go again. It's all very much a ceremony, a ritual – it's not for me.'

When I wrote that, I thought that going to church was pointless if that morning's experience was anything to go by. What I did not realise was that years of attending nothing but Kingdom Halls was preventing me from understanding the fundamental difference between Witness meetings and church services, namely, worship. Several more church attendances were needed before I could begin to understand this. And I had written in my diary, 'I won't go again'!

Shortly after this I had several discussions with another clergyman, met an ex-JW couple who had progressed even further down the road of Watch Tower Society investigation and discovery than I, and bought myself a non-JW Bible.

It was my new Bible which had the most profound effect on me. As I read it, no longer looking for justification for Witness beliefs, but openly seeking for the truth, passages about the deity of Christ leapt out at me. They were so clear it was as if they were printed in fluorescent ink! I was amazed, for although I was already familiar with those passages, I had never seen Christ's deity in them before. Also, the difference between this *New International Version* and the NWT was like night and day, especially when I compared it with the Society's Greek *Interlinear*. One of my ex-JW friends had studied NT Greek and went to great lengths to help me understand many of the crucial changes in the NWT which denied Christ his divinity and right to be worshipped. My friend encouraged me to go to the Baptist church as he and his wife had done. That turned out to be wise advice.

I felt at home with the fairly small local congregation of Baptists, about the same number attended as went to the local Kingdom Hall. Their services were grounded in scripture and worship. And their prayer meetings were, to me, phenomenal. The first prayer meeting I attended left an indelible impression.

The pastor, Mr. Guy Finnie, started the meeting with a reading and discussion of a passage of scripture. Then, mentioning individuals in the congregation both at home and abroad who might benefit from prayer for specific situations, he prayed briefly. In the silence that followed I looked up and found to my surprise that everyone else remained seated with their heads bowed and eyes closed. A couple of minutes later a man started to pray – his own prayer, about things which concerned him and other people. When he finished there was again a silence before someone else started to pray. This went on for about an hour. Women prayed too, much to my amazement!

I had never heard such prayers in all my life. They were the most simple, most sincere, humble and beautiful expressions of thanks, request and worship to God which I had ever heard. These prayers were spontaneous and unpretentious. They came from the heart. Some spoke eloquently with no hindrance; others haltingly and almost hesitantly. But each and every one prayed because they felt moved to communicate with God. And I noticed that many of the prayers were *purely* prayers of worship. God was not being asked for anything. He was being praised.

Never had I heard such prayers in a Kingdom Hall. No Witness ever stood up to say, 'Father, God, we praise and thank you and give you our worship for all your grace and glory.' I was beginning to think that the Witnesses did not understand the meaning of the word 'worship'. But these people here, in this rather cold, gloomy hall, made the air positively radiate with their humble offerings to God. At this point I will stop because words become inadequate. That night I experienced something most remarkable. I had been privileged to be amongst the people on earth worshipping God and Christ as is described in Revelation chapter five.

Prior to that prayer meeting, in the privacy of my home, I felt led to do two things. The first, on reading Philippians 2:9-11, was to do just what that scripture said, that 'at the name of Jesus every knee should bow... and every tongue confess that Jesus Christ is Lord, to the glory of God the Father'. The second, about a week later, happened on August 23rd, 1979. Inspired by Revelation 5:14 with its description of every living creature in heaven and on earth worshipping the Lamb, I offered my worship to him, and asked him to take over my life as Lord and Saviour. At first I could not do it. I remained on my knees for what seemed like an eternity, struggling to voice the words and feelings spinning inside me. Eventually, I managed to whisper what I felt was a suitable expression of this new-found devotion to Jesus, my Lord. No spectacular sensation followed, but within myself I felt a calm, quiet assurance that I had done the right thing.

I realised a lot of people would be thrilled to know of this step of faith and commitment I had just taken. Strangely, one person came instantly to mind, almost with a sense of urgency, Mrs. Hodgson. It was now nearly two years since I had last spoken to her. Impulsively, I reached for the telephone directory to see if I could find her number. The first one I tried was successful.

'Mrs. Hodgson?' I asked. 'You may not remember me, but about two years ago I had a discussion with you about the Trinity. I was one of Jehovah's Witnesses.'

She remembered me straight away. I told her that since then I had come to appreciate and acknowledge the deity of Christ. She was overjoyed. Many times after my visit I had been the subject of her prayers. I was quite touched. She went on to add that it was remarkable that I had telephoned her with this news just now, for in about a week's time she was leaving Britain for good to go to Australia to live with her daughters. If I had not contacted her then I might never have been able to at all, for she was spending the last couple of days with friends. What a remarkable piece of timing! She asked if I could possibly come to see her before she left and I gladly agreed. We had a lovely reunion.

Mrs. Hodgson told me that, prior to my telephone call, she had been asking the Lord for confirmation that her prayers were being answered. That was when I phoned. What confirmation! We were both staggered at the Lord's timing in all of this. The power of prayer was beginning to dawn on me, and not a moment too soon, for I then entered into one of the most trying and fearful episodes of my life; an episode which could only be resolved successfully by divinely answered prayer.

Pressure to stay
At this stage my family began to express their concern for me. My father wrote, warning me that my association with ex-JWs was 'dangerous'. I wrote back, sharing some of the things I had discovered, inviting his response and help. He agreed to consider the matter and to try to resolve my doubts. Then my eldest brother tried to help guide me 'back into the fold'. Even my husband expressed his dislike of the pathway I was so avidly pursuing. Although Derek was disenchanted with the Witnesses, he still had all their poisonous hatred for the clergy in his system. My increasing attendance at church displeased him, although he could not give any reason for objecting. And my in-laws next door blamed me for their son's 'falling away'.

Perhaps the most grievous burden thrust upon me was that of trying to help my father understand why I could no longer accept those things he had devotedly inculcated in me. He became a JW early in his married life, after the death of his firstborn son, aged five. JWs came knocking on his door, offering the hope of an earthly resurrection and paradise in the very near future. He and Mother, nominal Church of Scotland members, took in this message eagerly. I suspect their eagerness even went to the length of abstaining from having any more children for many years, in obedience to the 1938 edict of the Society.

The 1st November 1938 *Watchtower* had an article called 'Fill The Earth', which said that Armageddon was just ahead and the survivors would be privileged to then fulfil the divine mandate to fill the earth. Thus, the Jonadabs (a name for the newly 'discovered' earthly class of JWs) should not marry and rear children because of the urgency of witness work. On pages 323 and 324 the article categorically stated: 'It would therefore appear that there is no reasonable or Scriptural injunction to bring children into the world immediately before Armageddon, where we now are.' I remember father and mother talking about being in this 'Jonadab' class.[8]

My father was in his seventies when I explained to him my disenchantment with the Watch Tower Society. He tried his best to answer my questions but ended up simply repeating the passages from Watch Tower literature which had given rise to my queries in the first place. I could not help but wonder what kind of a dilemma I was placing him in.

My eldest brother also tried to get through to me, discussing matters in depth. In exasperation he once said, 'You could be an Evangelical Christian tomorrow!' In all innocence I replied, 'What's an Evangelical Christian?' Until then, I had never heard of them.

It was my brother who initiated the most disturbing process of disfellowshipment – before I was ready for it. Knowing I had attended church services and that he could not put me off my investigations, he advised me to ask for my record card to be removed from the congregation files. I did.

I also had another lengthy discussion with my elder friend, Dick, and the District Servant.

My statements in defence at that time were somewhat watered down, due to the conflict I was feeling between my convictions and my concern for family members. They responded by telling me at great length about their devotion to Christ, their honour and respect for him – the issues fundamental to my grievance with the Society. Then they warned me that I was in danger of becoming an apostate, hinting that my brother felt I was attempting to influence him.

When they left, I just cried and cried. They had succeeded in confusing me. It had taken me more than two years to form the conviction that Christ must be worshipped and now I was being told, in effect, that the Witnesses *did* worship Christ. Not, of course, to the same degree that others did, but they were imbalanced, not giving God his proper place, something the Witnesses felt they had always done.

I felt sick with despair. I had gone too far ever to return to what I had been before; a happy, zealous, enthusiastic and contented Witness. But now I found I did not have the nerve to break away completely! Would I really be launching myself into a sea of confusion and contradiction, as my family warned? I had been given the perfect opportunity to finally sever all connections with the Witnesses, but I had not been able to do it. Instead, I had ended up promising to 'think about it'.

A feeling of being under attack engulfed me. The previous month six different people had prevailed upon me with great earnestness and sincerity to remain a Witness. And the hardest part was that all these people were people I loved, respected and knew very well. It was hard – so very hard – to resist them. I wanted to agree with them, simply to keep them happy, to ease their anxiety, for they were so concerned for what they saw as my eternal salvation. For the first time in two and a half years I wished I had never started my investigations. If I could have turned the clock back to that Saturday morning in June 1977 I would never have knocked on Mr. MacKay's door.

The following week proved to be one of the most miserable weeks I have ever gone through. I was at a complete loss as to what to do next. I had no heart for studying; there was no-one I could talk to. Even whilst asleep I could not escape from my confusion for I had troubled dreams about being at meetings and going on the work. In fact, the idea of going back to the meetings presented itself seriously.

'Lord, I need some help!' was my anguished plea.

And it was just at that point that two things happened which helped me wonderfully.

Chapter 4

A Journey out of Fear

A particular fear which made me cling to the Witnesses, despite all I had learned and all the mistakes I had discovered in the Society, was that they might just, in some way, still be God's channel. Unreasonable though it was, I felt that rejecting the Society could amount to rejecting God's 'servant' and might place my feet on the broad road leading to destruction. How on earth I could still, at that late date, think of the Society in this way defies explanation. But it probably shows clearly how powerfully effective the Society's indoctrination is.

Being able to admit that fear had a hold on me was the first thing which helped me see the need to break free completely and officially. The second thing which assisted immeasurably was prayer. Realising I was in danger of giving up the fight, I went along to the prayer meeting specifically to ask the congregation to pray for me. I would be a fool to think I could do this in my own strength. So I briefly explained my predicament and the congregation included this matter in their prayers.

Within five days my mental conflict was firmly resolved because the most remarkable thing had happened shortly after that prayer meeting. Exactly how and when the realisation came to my mind I cannot say, but over those five days something dawned on me. If I *truly* believed in Jesus Christ's death and resurrection as the only means of salvation, then I simply *had* to depart from the Witnesses because they believe that an *additional* requirement for salvation is active membership in the Watch Tower Society. They have categorically stated that only dedicated, baptised JWs will survive Armageddon.[1]

If I believed – as the Bible so clearly teaches – that the *only* means of salvation comes through faith in Christ, I had to be prepared to stand on that alone. If I still clung on to the Society, it would be because of disbelief in the promise of Christ: '... so must the Son of Man be lifted up, that everyone who believes in him may have eternal life' (John 3:14-16). Jesus Christ was my Saviour, not the Watch Tower Bible and Tract Society. With that incredibly simple revelation clearly in mind, I knew the Society no longer had any hold on me.

With absolute confidence and happiness, I penned a letter to Dick, the elder with whom I had discussed my discoveries, saying that after thinking about his comments, I still could not agree and unless he could think of anything else relevant to the matter, I would like him to go ahead with the business of 'removing' me as a Witness. And, when the announcement was made to the congregation, could he please tell them that I still thought of them with affection.

Twelve days after I had posted the letter to Dick, he telephoned me. I could hardly believe my ears. He wanted to have another discussion. I thought the only event which would follow would be an announcement to the congregation that I was no longer a Jehovah's Witness, having clearly stated that my mind was made up. Yet Dick wanted to come over once more, but this time with a brother called Pat. I agreed, consoling myself with the thought that at least I would have another opportunity to witness to them about Christ. I would not water anything down this time.

Later that week they arrived, bringing a tape recorder with them. They explained that last Sunday's public talk at the Kingdom Hall had been entitled 'Recognising Christ's Central Position'. They had the recording of it and felt it would be beneficial to me. So, for the next hour we sat listening, and I took notes. The speaker dealt with four ways that JWs recognise Christ's role in God's arrangement:

(1) By recognising that the solution to the problem begun in Eden is in Christ (i.e. the ransom; 'Only JWs understand the ransom!')[2]

(2) By recognising Christ's role in prophecy (the entire theme of the Bible is Christ).

(3) By recognising that Christ set a personal example for us to follow (how closely do we emulate him?).

(4) By recognising that Christ is the foundation for all eternity (Christ is not just a letter-box to God).

As I expected, not one solitary word was uttered about worshipping Christ. This talk did not say anything different to what the Society had always stated about him. Dick and Pat wanted to know what I thought about the talk. So I told them.

'Look, Dick,' I began, 'I could spend hours enthusiastically extolling Jehovah's virtues, reading thousands of scriptures about his wonderful qualities, saying how much I appreciate all he's done for me. But if I stopped short of actually giving him my worship, it would just be all talk. It would be meaningless. And this is exactly the situation the Witnesses are in with regard to Christ. They can talk till they are blue in the face, but they are *not* worshipping him. Worship is a conscious, deliberate act of reverence. My brother suggested that I was actually worshipping my husband by obeying and respecting him. That is simply not true. Nothing would induce me to fall down on my knees or pray to my husband because those two things are acts of worship. In fact, if I was in solitary confinement for ten years, probably the only act of worship I could perform would be that of praying. Prayer is one of the most integral and basic forms of worship there is. But Witnesses refuse to pray to Jesus, despite the fact that in John 14:14 Jesus gave his followers permission to do just that; and the fact that the Society admits that Stephen's address to Christ was prayer; despite the fact that the first century Christians 'called on the name of the Lord Jesus'. Now, if I asked you what 'calling on the name of Jehovah' meant, I know full well you would answer that it meant *much* more than just talking about Jehovah or having benign thoughts about him, because Witnesses understand Acts 2 to mean that 'all those calling upon the name of Jehovah will be saved'. Jehovah is not going to save anyone who refuses to worship him. So, 'calling upon the name of' means using that name prayerfully and worshipfully.'

Again I accused the Society of polytheism, then asked, 'Now, what about John 20:28 – "My Lord and my God." Give me a satisfactory explanation for that, please. The "Aid" book's explanation is pathetic and completely fails to face up to the issues raised by that statement. And what about the correct translation of John 1:1? Everyone has avoided refuting the evidence that the NWT is wrong.'

Pat tried to state that many, many translations other than the NWT rendered John 1:1 similarly to the 'a god' translation of the Society. He did not get off with that!

'In the next room, Pat, I have a list of nineteen translations which say that the Word was God. Five more emphatically state the deity of Christ without using that exact expression. Nine translations do not clearly teach his deity and only the Watch Tower Society's translation outrightly denies that the Word was God.'[3]

In 1956 the Society condemned one Johannes Greber for translating his New Testament with the aid of communication with the spirit world. Yet they used his translation of John 1:1 to support their translation! This demonstrates how desperate the Society is to come up with any kind of support for their mistranslation.[4] The talk had said Jesus was a created being, basing this on the NWT of Colossians 1:15; '...the firstborn of all creation.' This was another mistranslation, I explained, in some detail.

Dick and Pat could not agree with my views. They again mentioned the subject of apostasy.

'Well, if to talk as I have been doing constitutes apostasy, then I would sooner remove myself from the Witnesses so that I can be free to talk. This is not something I can sweep under the carpet and seal my lips about, which is what I would have to do if I continued as a Witness.'

Eventually, I think I managed to convince them that I really meant to stop being a JW. But they wanted yet another meeting, this time with 'the Judicial Committee'! Only then could the decision be taken as to 'what to do'. Some people just cannot take 'No' for an answer!

'Dick,' I said, frankly exasperated, 'I don't need anybody's permission to stop being a Witness. If, as I have done, I formally request the removal of my card – in writing, signed and dated – then all that needs to be done is for someone to take the card out of the files.'

They explained that they were here today 'unofficially', with a view to 'restoring' me. I knew what that meant. According to Matthew 18:15,16, after two private attempts to put a matter straight with another who was in error, then the way would be clear to discipline or remove such a person if he still did not agree. They were obviously thinking in terms of disfellowshiping. If they would simply comply with my repeated requests, I would just gracefully depart before things got that far. But they wanted to play their game through to the end.

A charade such as this was enough to put most people right off their plans for leaving the Society. The fuss, bother and pressure would daunt even the most disgruntled Witness. To gradually become inactive and slip quietly out the back door is one thing. To stand up and say you are leaving is entirely another.

The final meeting was on Saturday 29th March, 1980, this time with a Judicial Committee comprised of Dick, Pat and another brother, James. It was held in the Kingdom Hall. For one and a half hours we talked, but *not* about doctrine. They were mainly concerned with my intentions to voice my thoughts. Did I intend to go along to church services and continue speaking to the brothers? I pointed out that I could not say what I was or was not going to do in the future, though I would not give the impression that I had no intention of ever going again to church, and that my speaking to the brothers had initially been prompted by a desire to obtain help. Since then, brothers had presented themselves to me, wanting to speak to me. I had not gone out searching for listening ears.

If they had hoped to hear me promise to keep my doubts and disagreements to myself, they were disappointed. But I had to impress on them that my leaving the Society was *not* based on church attendance or speaking out. Even if I never went to another church again or spoke another word, I *still* could not remain a Witness. My views about Christ were incompatible with theirs and I had no faith in the Society's claim to being the faithful and discreet slave. In such circumstances, to carry on as a Witness would be sheer hypocrisy.

They made a final effort to persuade me about the correctness of the Society's interpretation of Matthew 24, Babylon the Great, and the war issue, but I mentioned some alternative views based on scripture. James then went on at some length about the unity of the Witnesses. 'Where else can such unity be found?' he appealed.

'James,' I replied, 'since I've taken a stand on this issue about Christ, I've discovered many more

Witnesses who are very troubled about it but who dare not make their doubts common knowledge because of fear of being disfellowshiped. Their "unity" would not be so great if everyone felt free to speak their thoughts.' This caused some shock!

To their credit they expressed genuine concern for me. I thanked them but suggested they might do better to have more concern for other ex-Witnesses; the majority became sceptics, stopped praying, reading the Bible and worshipping. They ended up believing in almost nothing apart from the fact that there was a Creator. These ones appeared to have no consciousness of their spiritual need. Whether I was right or wrong, I had developed an even greater faith than before, and for the first time in my life felt the *desire* to worship God. That was something I had never experienced as a Witness.

Needless to say, my Judicial Committee raised the subject of apostasy as this was what they felt was involved. From the Witnesses' point of view this was understandable – I was clearly rejecting their teaching about Christ. Of course, from the *Bible's* point of view I was, for the first time, accepting its teaching about Christ! I was turning more to him. No way could I be accused of turning my back on him. If I had become a Muslim, or a Jew, or a Buddhist, then apostasy would be involved. But here was I, with an elevated view of Christ, greater respect and reverence for him than I had ever had as a Witness, and yet Witnesses suspected me of apostasy! If I erred, it was on the safe side. Surely it would be better for those on Judgment Day to be found guilty of giving Christ too much adoration than not enough!

As a result of that meeting I was disfellowshiped. The announcement to the congregation followed quickly. A baptised JW cannot hand his notice in – he has to be fired! At first my family and relatives did not react too strongly and for a few years I was able to visit my father and eldest sister. As they were forbidden to speak to me about spiritual matters I never raised that topic with them.

Then came the sad day when they both wrote requesting that I no longer visit them, and stopping all contact with me. However, my conscience would not permit me to ignore my elderly father as he did me. Very occasionally I travelled over to see him. This unspoken compromise seemed acceptable for the next few years. Then, the Thursday before Christmas 1988, came another letter from him. He simply said that because of my opposition to the congregation of Jehovah's Witnesses, he must sever his relationship with me and my family.

Cut off

Needless to say, such a letter arriving just before Christmas ensured a gloomy weekend 'for me. Initially Christmas had been a difficult time for me anyway; seeing families making special efforts to be together only reminded me of the great divide in ours, and although I quickly learned that many Christians celebrate Christmas without succumbing to the world's offensive excesses, Christmas is still very much just another day in the year for us. We remain the product of our upbringing in some respects.

Heavy of heart, I went alone to the Christmas day evening service but I was not really listening, distracted by despondency at my father's letter. Only Derek knew about it. With barely one ear attuned, I gathered the sermon was based on Isaiah chapter nine and on some of the titles of Jesus. But suddenly the pastor, Archie Macmillan, said something which emblazoned itself on my mind with all the force of a red-hot branding iron. He said, 'Even if our earthly fathers forsake and reject us, our heavenly Father never will, because he is "the Everlasting Father".' I realised instantly that the Holy Spirit was ministering to my deep, unspoken need. The comforting truth of that statement sank into my mind and heart and left me rejoicing. How I praised my dear heavenly Father for his awareness and timely initiative! He gave me the strength to shake off my feelings of rejection and continue walking forward with him. He is wonderful, indeed!

Strengthened and encouraged, I was composed enough to write a reply to Dad a few weeks later. I thanked him for all he and Mum, deceased fifteen years earlier, had done for me, and expressed the hope that despite any misunderstandings either of us might have we would both, one day, be part of God's congregation and family and thus be together forever.

I realised this could be my last communication with him. In a sense I had said 'goodbye'. Yet I felt at peace.

It was not really strange that my father and sister had tolerated my presence for a few years before severing all contact. In 1972 the Society wrote an article in *The Watchtower* called 'Abandoning the Course of Independence' in which they talked sympathetically about 'the condition of those who have gone astray', applying the parable of the prodigal son. Then, nearly ten years later, two years after I was disfellowshiped, they changed completely, cracking down hard on any kind of contact with those who leave the Society, irrespective of why they left, or whether they merely become inactive or are disfellowshiped. Though it took a while, first my eldest sister and then my father eventually succumbed to those dictates of the Watch Tower Society.

This new stance, as detailed in Society literature, makes for shocking reading. If I were to list the prohibitions and attitudes 'recommended' by the Society, most readers would probably not believe me. I might even run the risk of being suspected of maliciously misrepresenting the Watch Tower Society. Therefore, I devote space in another chapter to examining Witness attitudes to disfellowshiped ones, quoting extensively from Society literature.

It simply is not possible to understand how tightly JWs are bound by shackles of fear until one has a thorough grasp of what disfellowshiping and shunning mean in practice. Nevertheless, the shunning I received served two useful purposes:

First, it made me realise the tragic lack of love in the Watch Tower Society, because its type of shunning is a fear reaction. But 1 John 4:18 says, 'There is no fear in love. But perfect love drives out fear, because fear has to do with punishment. The one who fears is not made perfect in love' (NIV). If they truly loved me, they would not be frightened of me. I love them and only wish to pass on the good news of God's love in Christ. I am not frightened of (or by) them. The type of shunning the Bible mentions is reserved for those who once had the teaching of Christ but who reject it and, consequently, him. In order to justify shunning me, the Witnesses labelled me an apostate. Of course, this is all tied up with their fanatical conviction that the only true faith is the JW faith. I understand their thinking and actions and can only feel sorry for them that, upon seeing someone place all their faith and trust in Christ, their fear of such a thing compels them to shun that person as an 'apostate'.

Secondly, the shunning policy of the JWs had an effect on my husband. Derek was disgusted at the way former friends now treated me. And my own family's 'holier-than-thou' actions almost made him angry. It all served to ensure that his withdrawal from the Watch Tower Society became permanent. Despite the fact that he has never been disfellowshiped, he has been shunned just as much as I have been.

Discovering my sin
After the disfellowshipment, I had a long way to go before all the poison and fear inculcated into me vanished. Overcoming my fear of worshipping Christ turned out to be the key to dealing with all my other fears. It also proved to be the key to understanding the significance of sin.

Some time after my conversion, and after listening to more than a few sermons Pastor Finnie preached on sin, I remember sitting in the congregation one Sunday morning thinking to myself, 'Well, JWs may have a persecution complex but these people have a sin complex.' I was paralleling my Baptist friends' concern with sin with the JWs preoccupation with persecution. It seemed just as great – if not greater.

Then it hit me like a ton of bricks. How *dare* I criticize my friends' concern about sin when I had been so unconcerned about my sin of refusing to worship Christ! Yet again, the Holy Spirit was 'speaking' to me through a sermon. Suddenly, I had a glimpse of myself in my unconverted state, arrogantly telling others what to do to be saved from God's wrath at Armageddon, while deliberately refusing to bow my knee to Jesus. What utter blind folly to think I could please the Father whilst trying to bypass Christ with mere verbal declarations of my regard for him. No wonder God's response to my cry for help had not been to ease my depression but to cause me to face up to my disregard for the Saviour. The central issue in my two year struggle to leave the Society had been the deity of Christ – who *really* is Christ? – what claims does he have on me? – how am I to respond to who he is and what he has done? *This* was the 'big' sin in my life at that time. God revealed to me something of the glory of his Son, and the only fitting response I could make was to fall down in worship and adoration.

Seeing my pre-conversion resistance to worshipping Christ as sin which had to be repented of opened up the whole subject of sin in an astonishing way. No doubt most people think of sin in terms of stealing, adultery, murder and the like. That's how I thought. And because I could dismiss as relatively slight the 'lesser' sins I was prepared to admit as a JW, I never thought of myself as a 'sinner'. I knew I wasn't perfect, but my JW mentality conned me into imagining that because I subscribed to a certain set of beliefs and kept within the bounds of conduct stipulated by the Society, I would be granted God's pardon and favour at Armageddon. Sinners were people who had not come into God's clean organisation. Yet he showed me that sinners are those who have not grasped their utter inability to merit his favour, or upon making such a realisation have they sought his forgiveness. A sinner comes to that realisation by the grace of God, and equally by his grace casts himself upon Christ to be saved. What amazing grace, that God gave me the ability both to see and to do! He did this by revealing to me something of the deity of Christ. Until JWs realise their refusal to worship Christ is a sin of which they must repent, they will never know godly fear and remorse.

Fear of communion

The next fear to be tackled was fear of communion. I had been accustomed to observing this celebration once a year and had never partaken of the bread and wine. To find myself in a crowd of people who *all* took part every week was, to say the least, most disturbing. For a long time I sat through the sacrament without partaking. It took an ex-JW friend to jolt me out of my Witness orientated views. I expressed to him my feelings that those who were invited to eat and drink by Jesus were those who were going to heaven, those who were in the covenant for a kingdom. Since leaving the Witnesses I had no assurance of a 'heavenly calling' and it seemed presumptuous to assume that such was now the case. Dave kindly showed that my basic premise was wrong.

'Witnesses who partake of the emblems do so as

a declaration of their hope of going to heaven,' he began. 'But when Christ commanded his followers to remember him in this way, he said partakers had entered into a covenant for a kingdom. Even if the Witnesses were correct in their belief about the 144,000 and the other sheep, there is no scripture in the Bible which says the other sheep are not also "in" that kingdom covenant. They are still "in" the kingdom and are part of it even while on earth. Either being in heaven or on the earth isn't the point. Participation is a sign that one has put faith in the atonement sacrifice of Christ. To refuse to partake really amounts to a disregard for God's provision for forgiveness of sin.'

That shook me! The subject was now in an entirely different light and when I returned home to read the Gospel accounts of the Last Supper the truth of Dave's remarks became clear. Why had I not seen it before? '... this is My blood of the new covenant, which is shed for many for the remission of sins' (Matt. 26:28, NKJV). The forgiveness of sins is available to *all* who put faith in Christ: 'This is My body which is given for you; do this in remembrance of Me' (Luke 22:19, NKJV). Jesus' body was not just given for 144,000 people! I was not to wait for feelings of assurance about a heavenly calling – I was to act in faith, believing the promises of God. I *was* in that covenant for a kingdom, the new covenant. Partaking of the bread and wine would be an act of faith as well as of remembrance. The very next Sunday I attended the service and took the bread and wine. My acceptance of Christ as Lord and Saviour now seemed complete.

Discovering the Meaning of Freedom

Another area where discomfort can be keenly felt is that of spiritual freedom and slavery. Witnesses think that they are the only truly free people in the world. As they are the only people sticking faithfully to Jesus' word and are his only true disciples, they alone know the truth which sets men free (John 8:31,32). Everyone else, they conclude, is either enslaved to Babylon the Great or to the political 'wild beast' of Revelation. The great sense of reluctance to break away from the Society is often a result of fear that one might find oneself in bondage to something far worse.

However, the freedom which the Witness feels he has and the freedom which comes from Christ are vastly different. A Witness feels he is in a privileged, protected and safe condition just so long as he keeps within the restrictions imposed on him by the Society.[5] A follower of Christ, on the other hand, knows that his safety and protection have nothing to do with any organisation, or the lack of one.

But Christian freedom does not mean a freedom from responsibilities. Indeed, the sense of responsibility becomes keener after leaving the Society, for the individual can no longer depend on the Society to do his thinking or make his decisions for him. If he falls down on his Christian obligations and responsibilities, he cannot turn around and say, 'Sorry, Lord, but that was what *The Watchtower* said.' He can only look to Christ and seek forgiveness through the merits of his sacrifice. So his relationship with Christ becomes a reality, for he is an actual person to whom the Christian is accountable. And the lovely thing is that Christ treats the ex-JW as an individual; this is something he has never known in the Watch Tower Society.

Witnesses think that those who leave the Society, claiming a sense of great relief and freedom, must be indulging some long suppressed sinful desire or selfish ambition. For those who find relief and freedom in Christ, nothing could be further from the truth. As the ex-JW grows in grace, he learns how to exercise his God-given freedom for the benefit of others.

It took some time for all my fear to melt. Yet my flight from fear has been comparatively quick compared to others because I soon experienced the love of Christ during and after my departure from the Watch Tower Society. I became an adopted child of God soon after I left, and almost as quickly, the ties binding me to the Society were severed.

An ex-JW who has undergone the new birth needs to be shown the same love as an adoptive mother would give to a baby born suffering from the symptoms of drug addiction. Being expelled from the 'womb' of a cult is not enough. The cord needs to be cut and the newborn child of God incubated in a cocoon of love and Christian nourishment.

In the next chapter I will discuss three other issues which are sources of fear for JWs: 1914, assurance and blood transfusions, with the intention of letting Christians know how strong are the influences these three areas have on all JWs.

Chapter 5

Further Fears

1914 and other false beliefs
To Witnesses the year 1914 has the greatest obsessional hold. Many doubting Witnesses are prepared to risk holding on to the Society just in case the 1914 date is correct.[1] Pre-1975 JWs are particularly frightened at the thought of 1914 beliefs being changed.

Even now, with evidence becoming clear that the Society is preparing the ground to demolish its 1914 pillar and replace it with something else, most Witnesses are unaware of what is happening and refuse to consider the possibility that the 1914 date is on the way out. By the time the Society has slowly and carefully changed its position, a new generation of fresh JWs will have been recruited who have not been indoctrinated with the old 1914 teachings, who have never heard or seen the phrase, 'the generation old enough to see with understanding the events of 1914'. Twenty-first century JWs will have no idea that for most of the preceding one hundred years, Witnesses pinned all their hopes on Christ's second coming having taken place invisibly in 1914. Older Witnesses will either have died or will be too frightened to talk about it. Society literature will make selective quotes from old literature. Oh, yes, 1914 will sometimes be mentioned, and so will the idea that Christ's invisible presence occurred then, but it will be dismissed as a quaint burst of over-enthusiasm, something to smile affectionately about and promptly forget. This is just what has happened with the once cherished belief that 'Millions now living will never die'. President Rutherford rallied the faithful around that phrase, and they believed it literally. But see how easily the Society has dispensed with it in the 1st January 1997 *Watchtower*:

> 'In the early 1920s, a featured public talk presented by Jehovah's Witnesses was entitled "Millions Now Living Will Never Die." This may have reflected overoptimism at that time. But today that statement can be made with full confidence. Both the increasing light on Bible prophecy and the anarchy of this dying world cry out that the end of Satan's system is very, very near!' (p 11)

Whenever the Society is faced with the problem of dealing with a belief time that has proved to be erroneous, all it has to do is make light of it, then re-focus all eyes on 'the immediate future' and how near Armageddon must now be. This carrot-dangling tactic has worked nicely for over one hundred years and if any JWs dare to cast a worried glance backwards over the Society's track record of false beliefs, there is always the big stick of disfellowshipment hovering.

The Society is going to dispense with the problem of 1914 in exactly this manner. Already it has curtailed mention of it to a noticable degree. Whereas pre-1990 literature used to mention 1914 frequently, now it only comes up rarely. Even in the inside cover of *The Watchtower* magazine, which gives an opening paragraph stating the purpose of *The Watchtower*, and for decades boasted about their unique belief about the year 1914, all mention of it has now been dropped! In the above mentioned issue, the year is only mentioned twice in the entire 32-page magazine and on neither occasion is it linked to Jesus' invisible second 'presence'. In its 1996 brochure, specially designed for gaining recruits, *What Does God Require Of Us?*, the date 1914 is mentioned twice but again there is no connection with, or even mention of, Jesus' invisible second 'presence'.

What is becoming increasingly mentioned, however, is the coming 'Great Tribulation' when Jesus is going to come with the clouds and with the heavenly angels, in great glory. The Society has always talked a lot about the great tribulation period, but never before has it been linked with *another* coming of Christ which sounds identical to his 'presence' in 1914.

At the moment, all but the newest JWs think this will be a *third* coming because they still believe he came invisibly in 1914. When the Society thinks the time is right, they will casually mention this predicted event as being his *second* coming and get rid of the old idea that he had already come for the second time. Either that, or they will try to use scripture to prove that there is a sense in which Jesus can be said to 'come' a third time. Confusion will reign for a while amongst old JWs but they will have no choice but to accept the 'new light'.

Most JWs are oblivious to the way in which the Society manipulates their beliefs, as can be seen by present confusion about the tribulation. In an extensively used recruiting study book, *From Paradise Lost to Paradise Regained* (1958), the following clear statements were made about the tribulation:

> The great crowd has 'come out of the great tribulation.' This is the great tribulation or trouble that Jesus said would mark this 'time of the end.' This tribulation began on the Devil's organization A.D. 1914 when Jehovah's newly enthroned King took war action against his enemies in heaven. Jesus said that this tribulation would be cut short so that some flesh could be saved. How was it cut short? By God's stopping the war action up in heaven against the Devil's organization. So after the Devil was hurled down out of heaven the first part of the 'great tribulation' ended. Soon now the climax or last part of the 'great tribulation' will take place.... The last part of the 'great tribulation' means destruction of this world.... It is during this in-between period, between the first part and the last part of the 'great tribulation' on the Devil's organization, that the great crowd of 'other sheep' come out. Now is that time (p. 197).

For some fifty years this has been Society teaching. But that all changed with the 15th October 1995 *Watchtower*. First, the Society admitted they had been mistaken in teaching Jesus began to separate the sheep from the goats after 1914. They said the separating work was future, and would not begin until after Jesus came with the clouds, with the heavenly angels, in great glory, at the impending great tribulation. This in itself was an admission with immense repercussions which most JWs failed to grasp. They were being told that they could not know till then whether they were sheep or goats! They might be sheep-like now, but change before the great tribulation, and end up being cast into outer darkness. JWs never suffered from any kind of assurance about their salvation because they have no assurance, but with this change, what smattering of assurance they once clung on to has now evaporated.

So alarmed must they have been with changes to the separation of the sheep from the goats belief, they failed to spot the debunking of the *Paradise Lost* teaching concerning the resumption of the great tribulation. If the Society had been honest they would have admitted the old idea, that the tribulation started in 1914, was cut short for the separating work to be done and then would be resumed before Armageddon, was also an error. No such admission was forthcoming. The Society must have felt confident enough with preparing the ground earlier to assume that JWs had forgotten the old teachings. For example, two and a half years previously they had said: 'The *opening* salvo of the great tribulation comes with the execution of Jehovah's judgment on Babylon the Great' (1st May 1993 *Watchtower*, p.24, italics mine). Therefore, when I asked a JW in 1996 how she was coping with the problem of the tribulation beliefs, she said, 'What problem?' I explained it, then she said, 'Oh, we never believed *that!*' This was a JW who had been converted in the early 1940s! Even when she was shown the quotation from the *Paradise Lost* book, she insisted that it was all inconsequential and irrelevant. There was no problem. New light had just made things a bit clearer.

Three years later this Witness was reminded of what I told her in 1996 by reading the following belated admission in a *Watchtower* study (1 May 1999, p.16) article called 'Let The Reader Use Discernment'

God's people once understood that the first phase of the great tribulation began in 1914 and that the final part would come at the battle of Armageddon (Revelation 16:14, 16; compare with The Watchtower, April 1, 1939, page 110).

Although she eventually read this in *The Watchtower*, I hoped she remembered she heard it from me first! But before anyone thinks this is an encouraging sign of the Society mellowing by admitting to a mistake, the paragraphs following betrayed the Society's policy of casting blame on their members for not spotting their change to that interpretation.

Their next sentence read: 'However, in later years we have come to see things differently.' Were they referring to that 15 October *Watchtower*? Would they now come clean by spelling out the significance of their changed teaching on the separating of the sheep from the goats because of a future great tribulation? Oh no. They referred to a talk given by the then vice-president on 10 July 1969 at an international assembly of JWs in New York city. Not expecting any readers to remember that lecture thirty years previously, they obligingly quoted from the text. Yes, it appears an admission was made in 1969 that the old explanation was untenable and the great tribulation could not have started in 1914. It was still future. (The January 1968 *Kingdom Ministry* proves that the original teaching was still in vogue in 1968.)

Well, I was a zealous JW in 1969, being a Special Pioneer then, and I attended the London assembly at Wembley later that summer when the same talk was delivered. I don't recall any important change to end-time interpretation. Nor do I recall any other Witnesses mentioning this. How remiss of us! We couldn't have been paying attention over the four days of lectures.

Wisely the Society saw fit to remind their readers that thirty years earlier five sentences spoken by the vice-president spelled out this great blunder. The implication was that this erroneous interpretation was old hat and this 'significantly adjusted explanation' had been in place for thirty years.

Anyone who has sat through four days of monotonous droning at a JW assembly will realise why millions of JWs fail to spot such cunning devices for moving the goal-posts.

No wonder poor JWs are confused. Until they waken up to Society tactics they will keep thinking they are not being alert or studious enough to keep apace with 'new light'. The Society has a habit of dropping a few statements about changes to teaching, then not saying another word on the matter till many years later when they then quote the original passing admission to imply there's nothing new here.

Witnesses have such a plethora of studying, preparation and door-knocking to do, they cannot be expected to remember more than the bare bones of assembly talks. Nor have they got photographic memories to enable careful indexing of a few sentences in one decade to compare with contradictory views several decades later. They just thankfully and naively sit through Sunday *Watchtower* studies at Kingdom Hall doing their best not to appear forgetful or unaware of developments.

I know of three JWs who would have sat through the 'discussion' of that 1 May 1999 *Watchtower* article, not one of them daring to admit that a so-called 'apostate' had reminded them of what they used to believe three years before the Society openly admitted it.

No sooner had the changed teaching about the separating of the sheep from the goats been printed than another followed. It was about the generation which would see Armageddon. Non-JWs need to know that the Society has long attached a great deal of its authority on its interpretation of Matthew 24:34;

'Assuredly, I say to you, this generation will by no means pass away till all these things are fulfilled' (NKJV).

They have insisted that if they can identify the generation which sees all the signs described by Jesus in that chapter, they will know *that* generation will be alive when Armageddon starts.

This time, however, the changed teaching on 'this generation' was hidden amongst such convoluted material (in the 1st November 1995 *Watchtower*) that none but the most astute would notice it. The significance of this change would not become clear unless the Witnesses linked it to comments at the back of that magazine, in *Questions From Readers*, which was not a main study article. In a nutshell, the magazine abandoned old teaching about a generation being seventy or eighty years (but without actually saying so) by showing that a generation must be a comparatively short period of time, thirty-seven years being used as an example of the generation which saw Jerusalem destroyed after Jesus' prophecy in Matthew 24. It must be 'contemporary people of a certain historical period, with their identifying characteristics'. And it could only be identified with hindsight. Once the great tribulation starts, JWs will know *that* is the generation from which they expect to be saved. So if the great tribulation does not start for another forty years, then it is not *this* generation they need to be saved from (let alone the 1914 generation); it will be the *next* generation!

You are confused? Let me go back to the beginning and explain.

The Society has long experienced problems trying to calculate how long a generation is. The first President, Pastor Russell, tried to show that a generation equalled 36½ years, this probably being an average life expectancy figure of his era.[2] He was juggling with prophecies and felt a literal 36½ year period would snugly support his predictions. It didn't. He was quite wrong in all he said about 1914 and other dates.

So the Society changed this to saying a generation equals, at the most, eighty years. In the 8th April 1988 *Awake!*, p 14 they quoted from *A Greek English Lexicon of the New Testament*: 'Generation – "The sum total of those born at the same time, expanded to include all those living at a given time.'"

Based on the idea that a generation could be eighty years long, the Society gave itself eighty years from 1914 to see its predictions about Armageddon fulfilled. Before 1994 arrived, however, the Society caused itself major embarrassment by predicting Armageddon would be over by October 1975 at the latest. This false prophecy resulted in thousands leaving shortly after 1975, but now we are in the era of post-1975 JW converts who have not been told the whole truth about pre-1975 beliefs. They were, however, still being told that a generation equalled eighty years, and October 1994 was the deadline for that idea.

With the Society's back up against the wall of 1994, it was not surprising that they should produce a new interpretation of how long a generation is. Though it wasn't a new interpretation; it was almost exactly the same one as Pastor Russell's, minus half a year! What *was* new, was getting rid of the 1914 starting point for that generation. As the Armageddon generation will only be identified with hindsight – after the great tribulation starts – it is clearly still future. All the Society can do is insist it *could* turn out to be *this* generation we are living in. If Armageddon starts tomorrow, that will be true. What JWs need to face up to is that if a generation is about thirty-seven years then we are now three generations removed from 1914. Pre-1975 Witnesses do not care to admit to that.

It is worth knowing the above details if only to make the following point to JWs who appear on your doorstep. The Society keeps excusing their mistakes as, 'The light is getting brighter' (Prov 4:18). But there is a difference between the light getting brighter and the light being switched on and off. If the Society is applauding Pastor Russell's century-old views about a generation meaning 'contemporaneous people' (and coming very close to saying it is 36½ years in length), the light of truth has not advanced one particle. It means they were 'in the light' one hundred years ago, went into darkness for fifty years, and now have come back to the 'light' of last century![3] (For a detailed explanation of this complex subject, see Appendix.)

During my two-year struggle investigating the Society, Rogerson's *Millions Now Living Will Never Die* book played an important part in helping me see many such similar changes in belief. The list he provided of changes and about-turns was long enough then to show how futile their excuse was. In particular the pre-1914 beliefs about Jesus having come invisibly in 1874 and Armageddon due to end by 1914 shook my confidence in the Society very badly indeed. Now, Christians have an even longer list to present to JWs, and they should not hesitate in doing so. Although this in itself will not deter JWs, it will be invaluable in challenging the authority of the Society. If the light truly is getting brighter and brighter, as the Society claims, there can be no way it would ever go back to old abandoned ideas. Switching the light on and off is by no means confined to dates.[4]

Because most Witnesses are utterly convinced of the uniqueness and importance of 1914, this is a particularly good subject to have in mind when challenging them. As long as a JW harbours any conviction that the Society's teaching about 1914 is correct, he will not be able to break completely free. Wakening up to the nonsense attached to that doctrine was a great stride forward in my journey out of fear.

Assurance of salvation and good works

Another area of conflict needs to be addressed. It constitutes a real obstacle to any Witness coming to accept Christ as his Saviour and is labelled by the Witnesses as the 'once saved, always saved' attitude. They ridicule the notion that salvation is assured, considering any Christian who speaks confidently of his salvation through Christ as being self-righteous. Christians who have accepted Christ as their Lord and Saviour believe the words of Jesus, 'I give them eternal life, and they shall never perish; no-one can snatch them out of my hand' (John 10.28). They know that nothing can separate them from Christ. This confidence offends JWs.

To appreciate the Witness view of salvation we need to remember the difference between those who are the anointed (the 144,000) and those who have the hope of living forever on earth (the other sheep). The anointed are those who have the heavenly calling and who are declared righteous even while in the flesh. The other sheep are not anointed. Only at the end of the Millennium, when they have gradually attained human perfection, will they be granted everlasting life. Yet even the anointed, while on earth, believe they could lose their anointing if they become unfaithful to Jehovah or his organization before they die:

'To be brought to glory, of course, they [the 144,000] have to "do their utmost to make their calling and choosing sure," and they must prove *faithful* to death ...' (*Watchtower*, 15 Feb. 1998, p. 17 para 16).

'Suppose an anointed one became unfaithful. Would there be a replacement? Paul indicated as much in his discussion of the symbolic olive tree (Romans 11:11-32). If a spirit-begotten one needs to be replaced, likely God would give the heavenly calling to someone whose faith had been exemplary in rendering sacred service to him for many years' (*Ibid* p. 20 para 10).

In that case, they would never get to heaven. The other sheep, however, have from now till eternity to worry about slipping up and being annihilated since at any time they may fall sufficiently far short of God's requirements.

When a JW comes across a Christian who claims to be born again and is looking forward to being with his Lord in heaven, the Witness is not usually so tactless as to tell the Christian he does not believe he is born again. In actual fact, he is thinking in terms of this person being in exactly the same category as everyone else, someone whose greatest reward from God would be everlasting life on earth as a human if he becomes a JW before the great tribulation starts. In my days as a JW we dealt with this by trying to convince the person that only 144,000 people could claim to be born again. Nowadays some JWs have been reported as saying that they too are born again but that the vast majority of such ones will not go to heaven; they will live forever on a paradise earth. If any JW should take that line with you, it would be good to mention the article 'Who Are 'Born Again'?' in the 8th February 1988 *Awake!* which says only 144,000 people will ever be born again and all of them will go to heaven.

The simple truth is that JWs believe neither the 144,000 nor the other sheep can ever be assured of their salvation because it depends on enduring to the end and demonstrating good works till the day they die.

This is the point at which JWs totally misunderstand born again Christians who would agree that endurance and integrity are called for. This misunderstanding is due to their confusion about good works as opposed to endurance, and their inability to distinguish faith from self-righteousness. They have no assurance of salvation themselves and are bound to misunderstand.

Despite this, they can acknowledge the Bible's clear statements about the futility of good works alone. In their book *Make Sure Of All Things* (p. 439) when discussing salvation they list Titus 3:5 and 2 Timothy 1:9 under the heading 'Salvation Not Earned so That it is Due us: an Expression of Undeserved Kindness'. These scriptures read: 'Owing to no works in righteousness that we had performed, but according to his mercy he saved us'; 'He saved us and called us with a holy calling, not by reason of our works, but by reason of his own purpose and undeserved kindness' (NWT). A Christian would agree enthusiastically with those scriptures. In fact, when listening to believers praying, one is struck by their repeated expressions of amazement and wonder that

God has saved them from their sins through Christ. They cannot understand why God's grace has been poured out on them, unworthy as they know themselves to be.

It is because Christians are so aware that *only* faith in Christ can save them (Acts 4:12) that Witnesses jump to the conclusion that Christians sit complacently on their laurels rather than put their faith into action. In this they are making a big mistake. Witnesses also make the mistake of thinking that because certain passages of scripture, such as Philippians 2:12, say things like, '...work out your own salvation with fear and trembling', more is required for salvation than faith in Christ. They say they agree with the Bible that only faith in Christ saves but by their insistence that this is *conditional* on Christians working hard to demonstrate or prove they have faith, they show that they have not grasped the concept of salvation being a gift.

Christians, however, have such implicit faith in God that they know his promises will be fulfilled. There is no doubt in their minds (see 1 John 5:13, Phil. 4:3). They know that nothing they do can in any way assist in their salvation. They cannot 'by their... righteousness and holiness... at last have an accumulated credit with God and be richly rewarded for this' as the Witnesses believe (*Babylon The Great Has Fallen* p. 672). Despite having put faith in Christ Christians know they will continue to sin and be just as unworthy of the adoption as sons as they were before. The difference is that they trust God for forgiveness of their sins.

If I may put it this way, *proving faith versus*

knowing faith is perhaps the simplest demonstration of the Witnesses misunderstanding. In *Make Sure Of All Things* (p. 438) is the sub-heading, 'Faith Must be Demonstrated by Consistent Works'. A Christian would say, 'Faith *will* be demonstrated by consistent works.' A JW feels he has to *prove* he has faith. A Christian *knows* he has faith. This is not self-righteousness, rather a proof of the truthfulness of Paul's statement in Romans 8:16: 'The Spirit himself testifies with our spirit that we are God's children.'

James' letter shows that faith will have, as its natural consequence, good deeds, or works. Interestingly, the Society has brought out a commentary on James (the only commentary they have produced) wherein they state: 'James was not in any way saying that works of themselves can bring salvation. We cannot properly devise a formula or build a structure through which we can work out our salvation. The faith must be there first. As James clearly emphasized, good works will come spontaneously from the heart, with the right motive of helping people in love and compassion' (p. 6).

This statement, although it contradicts what the *Babylon* book said earlier, is fine in itself. But a few sentences further on comes the Society's definition of what constitutes 'fine works': 'So if a person has a genuine, living faith, fine works will reasonably follow, including preaching and teaching the good news of the Kingdom.' JWs believe that if a Christian does not preach and teach the Kingdom message about the coming millennium, then that person does not have a genuine, living faith. Going from door to door, talking about 1914 and earth becoming a paradise, is to them the real proof of a genuine faith. So, as they are the only people on earth preaching this message, everyone else professing faith must be either self-righteous in their works or not have real faith at all.

They cannot see that the prime concern of Christians is to tell others that only through Christ's death and resurrection our sin can be dealt with and disposed of. This is the gospel which the Bible preaches! JWs are so busy applying 2 Corinthians 4:4 – 'The god of this age has blinded the minds of unbelievers, so that they cannot see the light of the gospel of the glory of Christ, who is the image of God' – to everyone else, they do not even consider the possibility that it might apply to themselves. Blinded indeed, they cannot see that Christ in all his glory is God's way of salvation.

Christians place *all* their faith, trust and confidence in Jesus' ransom. JWs place *some* of their faith, trust and confidence in the ransom, some of it on working to prove their faith, and some of it in being active, baptised Witnesses. Until they have Christ alone as the foundation of their faith, and reject the Society as co-saviour, they will never know what it means to acknowledge him as their Lord and Saviour.

Blood transfusions

There remains one more great misunderstanding which gives rise to needless fear. This is the fear of accepting a blood transfusion. Since 1945 the Society described them as 'pagan and God-dishonoring' (*Watchtower* 1 July 1945, pp.198-201) and thousands of JWs have needlessly lost their lives. In years past it was impossible to ascertain any figures for deaths. The only source outside of the Society (which never published figures or even hinted at them to their members) was the news media. But very few cases have ever been reported by it. In hospitals where adult JWs sign legal release papers, any deaths due to blood refusal normally remain confidential.

Although sensational reports would occasionally grab the headlines, for many decades nobody could even guess at the number of deaths. But now – again thanks to the Internet – reports are flooding in. There is a site called 'Watchtower Victims Memorial' which makes for ghastly viewing simply due to the sheer number of (mainly) avoidable JW deaths over the years. This is but a sampling, the tip of the iceberg, because many people do not yet have access to the Internet or even know of such sites. Further, there are now far fewer deaths due to complications aris-ing from refusal to accept blood than in years past. This is due to sophisticated improvements in medi-cal procedures. It may safely be assumed that there were far more JW deaths decades ago than now. So, when we can randomly collate thousands of com-paratively recent deaths, it is no exaggeration to sus-pect many thousands more deaths going back to 1945.

One anonymous JW elder was reported as saying he estimates three JWs die every day 'so that the figures we are talking about are perhaps 1,000 Witnesses or more per year' (BBC Radio 4 programme *Sunday* 14 June 1998). He added that 'even discussing the subject has the potential to lead to expulsion from one's congregation'. When asked if his coming into the open and being named could lead to his expulsion he answered, 'Absolutely.'

From 1961 disfellowshipping became the punishment for those accepting blood (*Watchtower*, 15 Jan 1961, pp. 63-64). Again, it is only by examining God's Word and letting God be true that JWs, or ex-JWs, can be released from this fear.[5]

When still a Witness, there was a time when I was touched by this particular fear. It happened early on in my second pregnancy. During a pre-natal check, a nurse casually commented, 'Don't you feel a bit concerned, having a second child when you are Rhesus negative?'

Her words horrified me. No-one had told me I was Rhesus negative until that morning. Trembling with distress, I telephoned Derek at his work to tell him the shocking news. Immediately he made arrangements to find out whether the baby would be born jaundiced and in need of a blood transfusion by going to our GP for a blood test. If he was Rhesus positive, as are 85% of the population, then the baby could develop haemolytic disease, with all its implications. Even if I had been informed of the risk at my first pregnancy, I still would have refused preventative treatment in the form of a Rhesus immune globulin injection because it is extracted from the plasma of donated blood. My conscience would not permit me to have *any* blood product. Ironically JWs are now being 'allowed' to accept many treatments involving some blood products which were previously forbidden, e.g., organ transplants. At the beginning of 1967 they were denounced, but thirteen years later the Society gave the green light for Witnesses to have them if they wished. One wonders whether the day will dawn when whole blood transfusions will be accepted. All that is needed is an article to appear in Society literature saying 'new light' has been received on the subject.

However, back in 1972 I had to face the stark possibility of my second baby dying from lack of a blood transfusion. Astonishingly, Derek proved also to be Rhesus negative and the terrifying spectre quickly faded away. I often wonder what would have happened had his blood test shown him to be Rhesus positive.

JWs make every effort to present their stance as being reasonable and scriptural. Even in the face of adverse publicity when a JW dies, they minimise the situation, giving the impression that such things are extremely rare; indeed, there should be no reason why a Witness would die. When Nicola Geleff, aged 35, died after giving birth because she refused to accept a transfusion for haemorrhaging, the chairman of a north London JW liaison committee said, 'I know of no cases of this kind in which someone has died in Britain' (*The Times*, 22.3.91). The liaison committees work hard to appeal to doctors to accommodate their stance, providing them with up to date information on bloodless surgery, success stories and keeping twenty-four hour vigils by JWs bedsides, if this is deemed necessary to prevent a transfusion occurring.[6]

There appears to have been considerable pressure applied in the following case. The Melbourne, Australia, *Herald Sun*, 25th February 1998, had a front page article headed, 'Life Blood – A husband shuns his religious beliefs to win a legal ruling and save his wife's life.' The article said that a couple who had been baptised as JWs in 1997 allegedly signed over their medical power of attorney to a congregational leader. Although this was not legally valid, the pressure put on the husband to refuse his seriously ill wife blood was so great that days went past between her lapsing into unconsciousness and his seeking an emergency legal order to over-rule her previous refusal to have blood.

His wife had given birth to their first child on Friday 20th February 1998 but severe continued bleeding necessitated surgery. Prior to becoming unconscious she had refused a transfusion. Members of the JW congregation were reported as having gone to the hospital to tell the husband to abide by his wife's decision. His mother-in-law, also a Witness, 'allegedly pressured her son-in-law to abide by the religion'. An unnamed relative claimed that the husband 'agonised for days over the transfusion because he feared being ostracised by the church. He is scared they might retaliate against him.' It was not until Tuesday 24th February that the obtaining of a legal order resulted in the blood transfusion being given.

Despite a JW spokesman saying, 'We do not ostracise anybody', the husband is likely to face a judicial committee and be disfellowshipped. To be disfellowshipped is to be ostracised. Even if no such disciplinary action were to be taken against him his marriage may come under considerable strain should his wife continue to believe that transfusing blood violates God's commands. In *The West Australian* Saturday 28 November 1998, p.14, he was reported as feeling guilty nine months later. And his wife filed documents with the Supreme Court which has twice rejected her claim that the medical intervention was illegal. Her lawyers applied for special leave to append to the High Court.

Perhaps the best documented case of the length they will go to in order to prevent a transfusion was shown in the video, *Witnesses of Jehovah*, produced by Jeremiah Films. Paul and Jenny Blizzard refused a transfusion for their baby. So a Court ruling was obtained by the hospital, giving the doctors authority to administer blood. Before this could take effect JW elders urged the Blizzards to run away with the baby – even though the child would die as a result. At that point the parents realised things were going too far and refused to go. This caused the elders to turn on them and even though the Blizzards never gave permission for blood, the Witnesses treated them as though they had. They were ostracised. But neighbours and strangers showed the couple such love and care following their baby's treatment that the Blizzards became Christians. Some years later, when their child died, not one single Witness attended the funeral, not even relatives. This side of things is rarely seen by the public.[7]

The Society intermittently produces articles with emotive titles like, 'Doctors Tried to Take Our Daughter Away' (*Awake!* 22 Oct 1989), or, 'Selling Blood is Big Business' (*Awake!* 22 Oct 1990). In the former article a 42-year-old mother tells a harrowing story of fleeing from home in the middle of the night to escape a Court order to transfuse her week-old baby who had become jaundiced. After a 200-mile drive to two hospitals in another state, the parents told a doctor they would run away again if he tried to get another Court order. Perhaps the article should have been called 'We Tried to Take our Daughter Away From Doctors'. Because this story had a happy ending, with a photo of the beautiful three year old survivor, JWs would see nothing wrong with what happened, applauding it as an example of obedience to Jehovah being blessed.

The latter article had headings like, 'Gift of life or kiss of death?' and, 'That blood is a life-saving medicine is debatable but that it kills people is not.' After ten pages decrying blood transfusions the Society made this staggering claim: 'You may have seen newspaper headlines reporting that one of Jehovah's Witnesses died because of refusing a blood transfusion. Sadly, such reports rarely tell the whole story. Frequently, it is the doctor's refusal to operate, or to operate soon enough, that spells death for the Witness' (p. 12). Then they list 'A Wealth of Alternatives', asking, 'But if blood is dangerous, and there are safe alternatives to its use, then why are millions of people transfused unnecessarily?' This is followed by three short paragraphs mentioning their supposedly scriptural reasons for refusing blood. This seems disproportionate in view of their statement, 'Even if blood transfusions could be dismissed as the dangerous and unnecessary products of a frequently greedy industry, that still would not explain why Jehovah's Witnesses refuse them. Their reasons are altogether different and much more important.' If JW refusal to accept blood transfusions cannot be explained by medical dangers involved, but depends on 'altogether different and much more important' reasons, should not ten pages have been devoted to those reasons, and a mere three paragraphs to the supposedly insignificant medical dangers?

A perusal of Society literature on the subject of blood reveals a glaring inconsistency. The Society insists the only reason why JWs must refuse blood is because the Bible forbids it. Consider the following quotes from their 1977 booklet, *Jehovah's Witnesses and the Question of Blood*:

'Yet the stand taken by Jehovah's Witnesses is above all a religious one; it is a position based on what the Bible says' (p. 5).

'Thus the determination of Jehovah's Witnesses to abstain from blood is based on God's Word the Bible and is backed up by many precedents in the history of Christianity' (p. 16).

'The issue of blood for Jehovah's Witnesses, therefore, involves the most fundamental principles on which they as Christians base their lives. Their relationship with their Creator and God is at stake' (p. 19).

'The fundamental reason why they do not accept blood transfusions is what the Bible says. Theirs is basically a religious objection, not a medical one' (p. 49).

The bulk of their literature on the subject, however, is devoted to spelling out the myriad *medical* dangers involved, and only a small proportion mentions the biblical aspect. Indeed, the only medical aspects mentioned are dangerous ones. The Society *never* speaks of the benefits of having blood. They list the transmission of serum hepatitis, malaria, syphilis, cytomegalovirus, AIDS and anything else going, so that one could come away with the impression that all transfusions lead to the transmission of something obnoxious, if not downright fatal! This imbalance beggars belief. Why does the Society major on medical objections when no reasonable person can fail to see the benefits far outweigh any problems? And why does it mention medical objections at all if it is confident scriptural reasons alone will suffice? A look at the scriptural 'reasons' will show us.

Firstly, the Society quotes Old Testament texts which forbid the eating of blood. For example, Leviticus 7:26,27: 'And you must not eat any blood in any places where you dwell, whether that of fowl or that of beast. Any soul who eats any blood, that soul must be cut off from his people' (NWT – the following scripture quotes on the subject of blood will come from the NWT). 'Cutting off' usually meant being stoned to death.

However, an insistence that this law on blood should be observed would also mean an obligation to maintain the equally important law about eating fat, as demonstrated by Leviticus 3:17 and 7:22-25: 'It is a statute to time indefinite for your generations, in all your dwelling places: You must not eat any fat or any blood at all.' To the Jew the eating of fat was just as sacrilegious as the eating of blood. The penalty of stoning to death applied to both crimes: 'For anyone eating fat from the beast... the soul that eats must be cut off from his people.'

Secondly, this passage is part of the Mosaic Law, the Old Covenant, which JWs believe was abolished by Jesus' death. They are well acquainted with Galatians 3, Romans 7:6 and Hebrews 8, scriptures they use to show that other aspects of the Mosaic Law, such as observing a Jewish sabbath, are no longer in force for Christians. In their *Blood* booklet (p. 10) they *admit* that such dietary laws do not apply to Christians. So why cite them as if they constituted evidence for modern-day Christians who refuse to have a blood transfusion?

The one passage of Old Testament scripture which JWs can rightly claim support from is Genesis 9:4. This is the covenant God made with Noah, which was to apply to 'generations to time indefinite' (v.12) as opposed to the Leviticus 'generations' which applied only to the Jews. When Noah was given permission to start eating animal flesh, God added the stipulation, 'Only flesh with its soul – its blood – you must not eat' (v. 4). If *this* covenant has not been abolished, and the rainbow continues to be seen in the sky as the sign of this covenant (vv. 12-17), then the JWs are right in holding to the view that Christians are included in this covenant about not eating blood as food.

Interestingly, King David refused to drink water obtained at risk of his friends' lives, pouring it out on the ground (1 Chr. 11:17-19). Because his friends risked their lives obtaining the water, David felt it would be equivalent to drinking their blood and so poured it out on the ground because of his godly regard for the sanctity of life. That epitomises the spirit of the Noachian covenant. Blood is sacred because life is sacred. Blood is not to be treated as a mere food or drink. It represents life, and life is God-given. To risk life for a drink of water was unacceptable to David. Nowhere in the Bible is blood included in the category of food or drink. It stands apart and quite distinct from mere food. However, to go beyond this and say that blood taken into the circulatory system in order to save life is the same as taking blood into the digestive system as food is to go beyond God's written word. It is also to miss the point about the sanctity of life. It makes the sanctity of blood more important than the sanctity of life; something Scripture does not do.

Nowhere in his covenant with Noah did God say that death will be the punishment for eating blood. He does say, 'Anyone shedding man's blood, by man will his own blood be shed' (Gen. 9:6). To take a human life, i.e., to shed blood, is to take God's property: 'Look! All souls – to me they belong' (Ezek. 18:4). But if *no* life has been taken, no killing committed, yet blood obtained, will God require from man a life which he has *not* taken? Will God accuse a man of killing what he has *not* killed? If there is no killing, the law has no claims. The doctor who transfers blood from donor to patient does not kill the donor.

This leaves the JWs with only two verses to use, and they are both in the New Testament – Acts 15:29 and 21:25. Here the more vague expression, to 'abstain from... what is strangled and from blood' is applied to Gentile Christians. However, a closer look at the context lends perspective. The decree in Acts

15 was formulated because of the real problem Christians in the first century encountered in trying to prevent the Christian Jews from being offended and stumbled at the influx of Gentiles. The dispute first arose in Antioch where some Christian Jews said, 'It is necessary to circumcise them [converted Gentiles], and charge them to observe the law of Moses' (Acts 15:5). The error was thus pointed out and dealt with.

The Law of Moses, including the laws against eating blood and fat, had been fulfilled in Christ. Peter put the Christian view most concisely by saying, 'Now, therefore, why are you making a test of God by imposing upon the neck of the disciples a yolk that neither our forefathers nor we were capable of bearing? On the contrary, we trust to get saved through the undeserved kindness of the Lord Jesus in the same way as those people also' (vss 10, 11). No amount of keeping the Mosaic Law could save either Jew or Gentile (Rom. 7:6,7). Paul stated, 'Christ by purchase released us from the curse of the Law by becoming a curse instead of us' (Gal. 3:13). Paul continued, 'Consequently the Law has become our tutor leading to Christ, that we might be declared righteous due to faith. But now that the faith has arrived, we are no longer under a tutor. You are all, in fact, sons of God through your faith in Christ Jesus' (Gal. 3:24-26).

Such reasoning is quite simple and clear to us today. But in the first century it was an almost incomprehensible changeover with which many Jews could not come to terms. Some, like those men in Antioch, had the idea that Christians still had to be circumcised and keep the Law Covenant. So James informed them, 'Hence my decision is not to trouble those from the nations who are turning to God, but to write them to abstain from things polluted by idols and from fornication and from what is strangled and from blood. For from ancient times Moses has had in city after city those who preach him, because he is read aloud in the synagogues on every sabbath' (Acts 15:19-21).

The reason those requirements were laid upon the Gentile Christians was that from early generations Moses had in every city those who preached him, for he was read every sabbath in the synagogues. This decree was designed to pour oil on troubled waters, enabling both Jew and Gentile to come together in Christian fellowship. It was meant to show that circumcision was not the important thing any longer. Other things were more important. As Paul passionately declared, it was more important not to make your brother stumble than to stick to your rights (Romans 14:13-23).

Paul, almost immediately after the decree in Acts 15 had been circulated, found himself in company with Timothy, whose mother was Jewish but whose father was Greek. What was the first thing he did? 'He took him and circumcised him because of the Jews that were in those places, for one and all knew that his father was a Greek' (Acts 16:1-3). The very next verse says, 'Now as they travelled on through the cities they would deliver to those there for observance the decrees that had been decided upon by the apostles and older men who were in Jerusalem' (v. 4). The very decision which stated that Gentile

Christians were under no obligation to be circumcised! But if anyone was liable to stumble due to a Christian not being circumcised, then it was better that he be circumcised. The important point was that the newly circumcised Christian was not now bound to observe every detail of the Mosaic Law. His circumcision was purely a gesture for the benefit of Jews with a weak conscience.[8]

Similarly, the decree to abstain from blood was necessary in order to prevent Christian Jews from stumbling and to win over Jews to the Christian faith. If any Jew saw a Christian eating blood he would be so repulsed that he would never even begin to consider the Christian faith.

The blood issue is a horrible example of how sincere people can be fooled into thinking they can win God's approval by making martyrs of themselves. It shows how easily people can make the symbol for something more important than the thing it symbolises. Yes, the Bible says blood represents life and therefore is to be treated with respect. But when people lose their lives because they treat the symbol of life as more sacrosanct than life itself, they have lost more than the plot.

This imbalance is further shown in that no JWs have the fear of disfellowshipping hanging over their heads should they agree to an abortion for anything less than a life-threatening situation. Although the Society maintains abortion to be wrong, it has very little to say on the sanctity of embryonic and foetal life as compared with its emphasis on the sanctity of blood. A pregnant JW would strive to avoid a planned termination, but not at all costs. It is only when the threat of disfellowshipping arises that JWs place themselves (and their dependent children) on the Watch Tower Society's altar of blood.

The Society admits the soul is not literally in the blood but, 'Rather, the life of all souls is so inextricably tied up with and sustained by the blood in them that blood is appropriately viewed as a sacred fluid *representing* life' (*Awake!* 22 October 1960, p.15. Italics mine). It then tacks on a statement about the eternally life-saving blood of Christ to a sentence saying JWs hold on to the Acts 15:20 'law' because they want to obey their Creator. In this way JWs are encouraged to think that refusing blood shows such obedience to God that they will gain everlasting life if they die due to adhering to this supposed 'law'.

They have thus put the 'sacrifice' of their human lives on a par with Christ's sacrifice. The 'shedding' of human blood becomes a means of their gaining everlasting life, so they think. But any person who imagines that because he has refused blood his salvation is guaranteed, has missed the point. A Christian can *only* be saved 'through the grace of our Lord Jesus.' If only JWs could grasp the significance of that statement.

Debating theological aspects of blood will not, in itself, accomplish any lasting good with JWs unless the significance of the blood of Christ can be incorporated into the discussion. They need to see the futility of needlessly risking lives whilst remaining outside the New Covenant. How can he hope to please God by refusing a blood transfusion whilst also refusing to accept the merits of Christ's shed blood? He must be shown the dangers of not having Christ as his mediator and discover that Jesus is the only one mediator between God and men. This would therefore be a good place to start drawing his attention to his plight. (A group of JW elders are already using the Internet to try to change the Society's thinking on the subject of blood. See Appendix.)

Chapter 6

Seeing Fear For What It Is

'There is no fear in love. But perfect love drives out
fear, because fear has to do with punishment. The one
who fears is not made perfect in love. We love
because he first loved us' (1 John 4:18,19, NIV)

By now it should be apparent that JWs suffer a great
deal of fear and insecurity. Although they invariably
put on a bright, cheerful front, it is a mask. Their
seemingly optimistic outlook for the future is a raft
of badly misconstrued theology floating on a
quicksand of ever-shifting interpretations. Although
they would deny it vehemently many JWs know
within themselves that they are beset with doubts.
Being unable to voice them openly only adds to their
insecurity. Their fundamental reason for their fear is
that they lack the love of God.

It is important to differentiate between
comradeship and genuine, godly love. John's letter
is about the love of God which Christians have and
which, in turn, enables them to show love to their
brothers and others. It is *not* the same sort of love
that people who are in a closed community have for
each other because they think the rest of the world is
against them. The JWs thrive on a 'them and us'
mentality which results in a binding together and
mutual support. Non-Christians can demonstrate this
just as much in their clubs and societies. But the love

of God goes far beyond that. And there is a biblical test to determine whether someone claiming to be a Christian really has been made perfect in godly love.

Jesus said, 'But I say to you, love your enemies, bless those who curse you, do good to those who hate you, and pray for those who spitefully use you and persecute you, that you may be sons of your Father in heaven.... For if you love those who love you, what reward have you? Do not even the tax collectors do the same? And if you greet your brethren only, what do you do more than others? Do not even the tax collectors do so? Therefore you shall be perfect, just as your Father in heaven is perfect' (Matt. 5:44-48, NKJV). Only those who have been made perfect in God's love can do that. It is the unique hallmark of Christianity, perfectly exemplified in Christ on the cross when he cried out, 'Father, forgive them, for they do not know what they are doing' (Luke 23:34).

JWs are totally unable to show such love and forgiveness towards former members, branding them enemies and persecutors. They can only demonstrate a degree of love and forgiveness to those who show signs of returning to the organisation. It is a superficial form of love and conditional forgiveness, bearing no resemblance to the unconditional love Christ commanded in his followers.

This chapter will explode the JW claim to be the true Christian church by showing from their own literature its hateful attitude towards all those who dare to criticize it. It will show that the reason for its intolerance is fear, *not* obedience to God's commands to shun apostates, because even if some of the people they shun truly were apostates, the vast majority can by no stretch of the imagination be made to fit the description of apostates or antichrists, even by the Society's own standards. The unloving and unchristian motives behind Society shunning policies will become clear.

The reason JW love is superficial is because only 0.157% of them claim to be indwelt by the Holy Spirit, and of that tiny percentage, some are directly responsible for Society shunning policies, which casts severe doubts on their claims. John explained, '...if we love one another, God lives in us and his love is made complete in us. We know that we live in him and he in us, because he has given us of his Spirit' (1 John 4:12,13). Perfect love – God's love – can only be experienced and shown by those who have God's Holy Spirit living in them. Although JWs insist they *all* 'have' God's holy spirit, when pressed, they have to confess that only 8,755 JWs presently claim to have God living in them by the holy spirit. The five and a half million other JWs have been told they will only have as much of the holy spirit as they 'deserve' by study and obedience. If they study really hard and are really obedient, they will have greater access to the holy spirit than less diligent Witnesses. As we have already seen, such spiritual apartheid is not of God. One is either indwelt by the Holy Spirit, or one is not (2 Cor 13:5; John 3:34). If those who claim to be anointed JWs loved their brothers they would not try to prevent them from becoming true children of God.

John said in his letter, 'Dear children, let us not love with words or tongue but with actions and in truth' (1 John 3:18). If the anointed JWs loved their brothers 'in truth', they would not forbid their brothers the right to enquire into truth. Instead of saying, 'The truth is disseminated by us, and us alone,' they would admit the truth of 1 John 2:26,27: 'I am writing these things to you about those who are trying to lead you astray. As for you, the anointing you received from him remains in you, and you do not need anyone to teach you. But as his anointing teaches you about all things and as that anointing is real, not counterfeit – just as it has taught you, remain in him.'

It is the Holy Spirit who teaches, not a select group of men. It is worth noting that in 1999 only thirteen of the 8,755 anointed JWs do any teaching in the organisation. Others only repeat what they are told to teach by this elite leadership core. It is the Governing Body, based in New York, which determines what will be taught. They do not even know who the other anointed JWs are outwith their own circle of acquaintance. There is no list of names of the anointed. Branch Offices do not know. Articles submitted by other JWs are far more likely to be written by those of the other sheep than the anointed. And the Governing Body controls everything submitted, editing it. Others of the anointed may be elders in congregations, but they do not teach; they merely repeat what the Governing Body says. So when thinking about the role of teachers in the Society, it is important to remember just how select that little group is. It is round about a dozen men.

This tiny group retains total authority over five and a half million JWs, giving them immense control in a massive organisation. As long as JWs believe them to be 'the faithful and discreet slave' these leaders remain unchallenged and their every word is obeyed. With over one hundred years of such heady power behind them, they are not likely to change their strategy now.

Yet the thought of their deception being discovered by the rank and file must fill them with great fear. This is why they blacken the name of all who leave the movement, classifying those who commit unchristian behaviour with those who become evangelical Christians. By doing this, they hope to create such distaste for all who leave that no enquiry will be made of ex-JWs. I say 'ex' because all JWs who become Christians due to acknowledging Jesus Christ as their Saviour and Lord seem to leave. Even if they wanted to stay, their elevated estimation of Christ would lead to their removal.

The shunning policies also major on punishment, creating great fear of the punishment of shunning and it is this fear rather than love that binds many to the organisation. Christians know they have passed over from judgment to life and experience the forgiveness of God but JWs have still to face the judgment of God and, not surprisingly, the fear of punishment is very real.

What happened to five million JWs?

Thousands of JWs have left the Society because they experienced the leading of the Holy Spirit. Therefore the Governing Body is desperate to stem the flow. It has been calculated that over one quarter of a million left in 1977 and 1978 alone. The 1977 annual service year report showed that the number of Witnesses decreased by 21,243 even though 124,459 new ones were baptised. The 1978 report showed a decrease of 30,496 (1.4%) despite 95,052 new Witness baptisms. This was 29,407 less than in 1977 – a 23% decrease in baptisms. A total of 271,250 Witnesses left during those two years. And they did not all die! I think the majority left because they realised the prediction that Armageddon would come in 1975 was a false prophecy.

Nearly ten years later came this admission from the Society:

> Shocking as it is, even some who have been prominent in Jehovah's organization have succumbed to immoral practices, including homosexuality, wife swapping and child molesting. It is to be noted, also, that during the past year, [1985] 36,638 individuals had to be disfellowshipped from the Christian congregation, the greater number of them for practicing immorality (*The Watchtower* 1 January 1986, p.13).

The haemorrhage after 1975 had been stemmed to a degree but the numbers put out in the 1980s continued to be significantly high, as in the example above. Readers of *The Watchtower* are never encouraged to query what proportion of those disfellowshipped go on to worship God as professing Christians. Do not forget either that many more JWs slip out the back door without being disfellowshipped.

The 1990s showed little improvement. In Britain, the 1996 figures showed a -0.4% decline in members. As 4,758 people were baptised, around 5,000 must have left the movement. Apart from 1995, the trend has been for smaller growth over the last few years. This is also reflected in the worldwide statistics. If we start with the 1990 peak publisher figure, add those baptised between 1991 and 1995 and compare this with peak publishers in 1996, there are some 13,000 British publishers missing and a total of 150,000 worldwide.

Every year thousands of Witnesses leave. Some have even calculated that over five million have left in the past thirty years. By no means all of them left because they became Christians, but scores of thousands did! The Society does not want its members considering the implications of such a startling reversal which undermines its teaching that by the mid-1930s the full number of the anointed had been reached and the newly 'identified' great crowd would increase to millions with the anointed simultaneously declining. For decades statistics appeared to confirm this idea:

Year	No. Attending Memorial	No. Partaking of Emblems
1935	63,146	52,465
1965	1,933,089	11,550
1995	13,147,201	8,645

As long as figures confirmed their expectations the Society did not have a problem, dismissing the thousands who left as backsliders or apostates. If any of them managed to tell JWs they were not backsliders or apostates but evangelical Christians, they were simply disbelieved. And very few who became Christians were even able to speak to JWs because of the shunning tactics. Because the Society publicised the supposed immorality and worldliness of all those who 'abandoned true worship', the idea that thousands were now Christians was a non-starter. It seemed that the problem had been disposed of quietly.

But from 1993 something strange began to happen to the memorial partakers' statistic. At first it looked like a little hiccup. Ten more people partook than in the previous year. In 1994 all was well again as the partakers had decreased by a comfortable 76. Things were back on course. Then came 1995, and 28 more partook than in 1994. Still, the ratio of partakers to those attending did drop and the Society gave this soothing explanation to a question about such an unexpected aberration:

[Question] 'The reports for some years show that the number partaking of the Memorial emblems increased slightly. Does this suggest that many new ones are being anointed with holy spirit?' [Answer] 'There is good reason to believe that the number of 144,000 anointed Christians was complete decades ago...

At the Memorial celebration in our time, the speaker often calls attention to the apostle Paul's words at Romans 8:15-17, which mention that the anointed 'receive a spirit of adoption as sons'.... Those who truly have this Spirit-anointing know it with certainty. It is not a mere wish or a reflection

137

of an emotional and unrealistic view of themselves.

...But it seems that in the mid-1930s, the full number of the 144,000 was basically completed. Thus there began to appear a group of loyal Christians with the earthly hope.

...The most recent published report is for the year 1995, and it shows 28 more partakers than in the preceding year though the ratio of partakers to those attending did actually drop. On balance, that a few more chose to partake of the emblems is no cause for concern. Over the years some, even ones newly baptized, have suddenly begun to partake. In a number of cases, after a while they acknowledged that this was an error. Some have recognized that they partook as an emotional response to perhaps physical or mental strain. But they came to see that they really were not called to heavenly life. They asked for God's merciful understanding. And they continue to serve him as fine, loyal Christians, having the hope of everlasting life on earth.

There is no need for any of us to be concerned if a person begins to partake of the emblems or ceases to do so. It really is not up to us whether someone actually has been anointed with holy spirit and called to heavenly life or not... There is every reason to believe that the number of anointed ones will continue to decline as advanced age and unforeseen occurrences end their earthly lives. Yet, even as these truly anointed ones prove faithful till death, in line for the crown of life, the other sheep, who have washed their robes in the blood of the Lamb, can look forward to surviving the impending great tribulation' (*The Watchtower* 15 August 1996, p 31 'Questions From Readers').

Alas, despite assuring Witnesses that 'there is every reason to believe that the number of anointed ones will continue to decline', the opposite happened the following year. 1996 saw 112 more partaking than in 1995! Then in 1997 38 more JWs partook than in 1996. This meant that over five years an average of 112 more Witnesses identified themselves as being anointed. Comparing this modest amount with the hundreds of thousands who would claim to be truly anointed since leaving the JWs, it would seem absurd that the Society felt obliged to write an article explaining away 28 more claimants for the anointing almost as soon as other Witnesses noticed it, whilst refusing to acknowledge such claims by hundreds of thousands of ex-JWs over many years. What will the Society do now that 112 more have identified themselves? Will this merit a study article in *The Watchtower* which all five and a half million JWs have to go through on Sunday mornings? And what tactics will the Society adopt to dissuade them from partaking in future years? Subtle hints about wishful thinking or an emotional and unrealistic view of themselves clearly are not enough. Might this produce firm teaching from the Society that John 1:12,13 should have said, '144,000' instead of 'all', or something else of that kind? (See Appendix for evidence of just such firm teaching.)

Although this might strike Christians as absurd, it serves a very useful purpose as it shows what frightens the Society. They are not frightened by hundreds of thousands leaving and many of those ones claiming to be spirit-anointed because they have a method for dealing with that which seems to be working. But let 28, or 112 or more begin taking the emblems at the Memorial, and a problem arises which threatens to undermine their fundamental teaching.

Year	Memorial Partakers
1994	8,617
1995	8,645 = 28 more than previous year
1996	8,757 = 112 more than previous year and 140 more than 1994
1997	8,795 = 38 more than previous year and 150 more than 1995
1998	8,756 = 39 less than previous year but still 111 more than 1995
1999	8,755 = 1 less than previous year but 110 more than 1995 **and 138 more than 1994**

Irrespective of how many Witnesses partake of the emblems, it is certain that Spirit-anointed JWs will not thrive in a community which tries to control and suppress God's calling and election.

How those who leave, or are put out, are viewed
Let us now go back to the way the Society has dispensed with the problem of hundreds of thousands of JWs leaving. Very many leave because they cannot cope with the pressures, others commit adultery or bring the Society into disrepute by some illegal action.

They might also have been found smoking which is a disfellowshipping offence if baptised and if not, then inability to stop smoking will debar that person from baptism. Or they may have accepted a blood transfusion or permitted one for a dependent. But a considerable number have committed no such 'sins'. They have simply given more honour to Christ than the Society permits.

In the following extracts remember that 'those who have gone astray', 'the disfellowshiped' or 'expelled' people referred to, include this immensely disparate group of people.

'The condition of those who have gone astray.... All such persons are spiritually famished and far removed from Jehovah God, as if in a distant country. They are a part of Satan's world and in slavery to him. While many who are no longer associating with God's people [i.e. JWs] may not be leading a debauched life, they have, nevertheless, lost much. Devoid of spirituality, their life is often one of constant frustration. Not infrequently does their desire to get ahead in the world lead them to adopt dishonest business practices' (*The Watchtower* 15 July 1972, p. 433).

'The expelled person.... has known the way of truth and righteousness, but he has left that way and unrepentantly pursued sin to the point of having to be expelled.... Hence, out of love Christian elders and others might visit and help the one who has grown weak and inactive.... It is another matter, though, when a person repudiates his being a Christian [?] and disassociates himself.... When this rare

[?] event occurs, the person is renouncing his standing as a Christian [?], deliberately disassociating himself from the congregation.... Or, a person might renounce his place in the Christian [?] congregation by his actions, such as by becoming part of an organization whose objective is contrary to the Bible [any Christian denomination, for example], and, hence, is under judgment by Jehovah God.... Persons who make themselves 'not of our sort' by deliberately rejecting the faith and beliefs of Jehovah's Witnesses should appropriately be viewed and treated as are those who have been disfellowshiped for wrongdoing.... Should [JWs] say 'Hello' or even chat briefly if they cross paths with the expelled person? What about working for him or hiring him? To what extent should Christian [?] parents, or other relatives, communicate or keep company with the individual?... Hence, the Bible here rules out social fellowship, too, such as joining an expelled person in a picnic or party, ball game, trip to the beach or theatre, or sitting down to a meal with him' (*The Watchtower*, 15 September 1981, pp. 17, 22, 23, 24).

Concerning expelled relatives we read:

'For example, if the husband is disfellowshiped, his wife and children will not be comfortable with him conducting a family Bible study or leading in Bible reading and prayer. If he wants to say a prayer, such as at mealtime, he has a right to do so in his own home. But they can silently offer their own prayers to God.... What if a disfellowshiped person in the home wants to be present when the family reads the Bible together or has a Bible study? The others might let him be present to listen if he will not try to teach them or share his religious ideas.... For example, a Christian [i.e. a JW] couple might be getting married at a Kingdom Hall. If a disfellowshiped relative comes to the Kingdom Hall for the wedding, obviously he could not be in the bridal party there or 'give away' the bride. What, though, if there is a wedding feast or reception? This can be a happy social occasion.... But will the disfellowshiped relative be allowed to come or even be invited? If he was going to attend, many Christians [i.e. JWs] relatives or not, might conclude that they should not be there, to eat and associate with him, in view of Paul's directions at 1 Corinthians 5:11. Thus, sometimes Christians [i.e. JWs] may not feel able to have a disfellowshiped or disassociated relative present for a gathering that normally would include family members... Should he die while disfellowshiped, arrangements for his funeral may be a problem. His Christian [i.e. JW] relatives may like to have had a talk at the Kingdom Hall, if that is the local custom. But that would not be fitting for a person expelled from the congregation... even such a talk [at the funeral home or grave side] would not be appropriate' (*Ibid*, pp. 28, 30, 31).

What a horrifying list of do's and don'ts! Where, in the Bible, is there any such catalogue of rules and regulations governing Christians? And is it not also striking that every single person who has been disfellowshiped or who has left the Society is to be treated the same way? Someone who is put out for smoking is shunned with equal fervour as one who commits adultery or who claims to have become an evangelical Christian![1]

The only 'concession' to degree of 'sin' was hinted at in the answer given to a *Watchtower* reader who asked this question: 'Would it ever be in order to pray regarding someone who has been disfellowshiped from the Christian congregation?' The answer first admitted that: 'In the past it has been held that such prayers would not be proper.' But now the 'suggestion' was that as only God can determine whether someone has sinned against the holy spirit ('for which there is no forgiveness'), it might be possible to pray for someone who, after expulsion, showed signs of repenting, the assumption being that a lack of repentance proved that the unforgivable sin *had* been committed! Yet such prayers for a person appearing to repent must never be congregational or public. The reason? '...others hearing such prayers may not yet know of the evidence indicating repentance. Or they may not yet be convinced that the person has not committed a "sin that does incur death".'

Is this not amazing? In one breath it is acknowledged that only God can determine whether the holy spirit has been sinned against, then in the next, congregation members who suspect an expelled person of just such a gross sin must not be offended by congregational prayer for that person! This shows that an expelled person is not innocent until proven guilty of having sinned against the holy spirit, he is assumed guilty until showing signs of repenting (even though he may *not* have sinned against the Holy Spirit!). It also shows a proud refusal to acknowledge the possibility that the person might have been expelled unfairly. The answer also made this emphatic statement:

'...we should not pray in behalf of a person who gives evidence of practicing sin deliberately. John also wrote in 2 John 9–11 about persons who spread unchristian views. Prayers in their behalf would be offensive to God' (*The Watchtower*, 15 October 1979, p. 31).

The scripture referred to does *not* forbid prayers. Let it also be noted that 'spreading unchristian views' means talking about the worship of Christ, the reality of hell as a place of punishment, the numerically unlimited availability of the Holy Spirit to 'all who believe' in Christ etc. In short, JWs are told not to pray for anyone who used to be a Witness but who now dares to speak about any belief the Society says is wrong.

One-sided evidence
Society attitudes since 1979 have become even more rigid. The April 15 1988 *Watchtower* contained an article exploiting a court action brought against the Society by a woman who was claiming damages for being shunned. The case was rejected by the US Supreme Court. Despite the article admitting that the case failed because '...courts do not get involved in church disciplinary matters', the Society used this 'victory' as evidence that their actions were right. It quoted an instance of a case where shunning had the desired effect on a girl called Margaret. Because her JW sister, Lynette, stopped association with her, Margaret returned to the Society. The Society publications *never* report cases where shunning causes the opposite reaction.

Everything in Society literature is a justification of its beliefs. Contrary evidence is either edited to such an extent that all the negative evidence has been removed or, if that is not possible, it is outrightly banned.

The 15 March 1986 *Watchtower* had an article which attacked material critical of the Society. It said that any written criticism of the Governing Body would be written by apostates. It should not be read. Alongside was a photograph of a good JW woman following the Governing Body's instructions. With a suitably grim expression on her face, she was putting such literature straight into the waste-bin, unread. The postman had only just left her doorstep. The caption read, 'Do you wisely destroy apostate material?'

The Watch Tower Society applauded Government court action which prevented their literature from being banned during the Second World War, but it does not hesitate to ban literature which dares to criticise it. Freedom of the press is only tolerated as long as the Watch Tower Society receives a good press.

At the back of all this censorship is fear. In order to ensure that Witnesses keep their unquestioning place, the dozen or so leaders have instilled fear into them – fear of disobeying the Governing Body's decrees. They have been told that if Armageddon comes while they are outside Jehovah's organisation they will die a judgmental death, never to be resurrected. This fear of not passing the test of Armageddon is very great, so great that many who have serious doubts regarding the Society's claims are prepared to stifle their apprehension 'just in case'.

Yet even the most conscientious, totally devoted to obeying the Governing Body's every edict, cannot be absolutely certain that they will survive. JWs quote with great seriousness Zephaniah 2:3, 'Seek Jehovah, all you meek ones of the earth, who have practiced his own judicial decision. Seek righteousness, seek meekness. Probably you may be concealed in the day of Jehovah's anger' (NWT). Their chances of surviving Armageddon are no more than a probability.

Yet the very thing they *should* fear, the Day of Judgment, is treated with light-hearted optimism. Romans 6:7 is used to 'prove' that: '...at death a person is set free from any sins he has committed. This means that when a person is resurrected he will be judged on the basis of what he does during Judgment Day, not what he did before he died' (*You Can Live Forever In Paradise On Earth* p. 175 para 3). In order to support this misconception, JWs have to ignore the many scriptures which refer to people being judged for what they have done (past tense). They do this by saying Judgment Day will be a thousand year period (*ibid* p. 180 para 13), so judgment will be rendered according to what people do during that millennium.

Even Witnesses who survive Armageddon will be judged on their actions during the 1,000 years after it (*ibid* p. 181 para 16). Therefore, surviving Armageddon is not the only worry for present day Witnesses. If they clear that hurdle they still have a thousand-year testing period to follow. *Then* will come Satan's release and a final attempt to lure people away from God. If any Witness succumbs to Satan he will die and be annihilated. Fortunately, all this is too much in the realms of the distant future to be real to JWs. They occasionally speculate about it, but think their continued obedience now will give them some kind of accumulated merit and conclude that they will have an excellent chance of getting through the millennium intact.

This end-time theology means that the Day of Judgment becomes, simply, a millennium of paradise-like pleasure. On pages 176 and 177 of this *Paradise* book, beautiful illustrations of wonderful earthly scenes are featured. Paragraphs 5 and 6 say: 'Look at these pages. They give some idea of how wonderful Judgment Day will be for humankind. During Judgment Day those who survive Armageddon will work to make the earth a paradise. Into this paradise the dead will be welcomed back.... Yes, how pleasant to live in peace, to enjoy good health and to receive instruction regarding God's purposes!'

This is expected to be the happy lot of people who enter the Day of Judgment with all their sin remaining. They will not have had it dealt with and disposed of before then. They will not be able to say, 'My life is now hidden with Christ in God' (Col 3:3). They will be trusting in their obedience to a few men in America, on their high moral standards, on their sacrifices to attend meetings and go on the work – anything, in fact, except faith *alone* in the sacrifice of Christ.

'On Christ the solid rock I stand, all other ground is sinking sand.' So goes the chorus of a well known hymn. No JW ever sings those lines, and their frenetic activity shows why they cannot.

148

Their own *Paradise* book says about the Day of Judgment, 'It will be more difficult for those who personally rejected Jesus' (p.179 para 10). Little do they realise that by remaining outside the New Covenant they have, in effect, done just that. Every year, as they pass the bread and the wine around without partaking of these blessed elements, without even *desiring* to have Christ as their High Priest, they come closer to hell, rejecting Christ because of the gross deception that blinds them.

Who is going to tell them about the reality of a lost eternity which will be even more dreadful than the soul annihilation they preach? Who is going to awaken them to the realities of the Day of Judgment? Christians have the privilege and obligation to confront them with the gravity of their situation. How best can this obligation be discharged?

Chapter 7

There is No Fear in Love

Nancy noticed it had been a long time since JWs last called at her home. She prayed about it. 'Lord,' she asked, 'Send some Witnesses to my door, so that I may share the gospel with them.' Shortly afterwards there came a knock at the door. Two little girls stood on her doorstep, *The Watchtower* and *Awake!* magazines in hand. 'Surely I'm not meant to witness to such young children?' Nancy thought. She asked them to bring an adult over. A little later a young JW man arrived and gladly agreed to come back with his wife at a later date.

Although Nancy prepared for the visit it was not long before she was totally out of her depth. The couple had her tied up in knots as they flitted back and forth through the Bible, jumping from one passage to another.

It would have been perfectly understandable if Nancy, at that point, had said, 'Lord, you answered my prayer and I did what I could. It's over to you now.' Instead, she agreed to a return visit, before which she opened her Bible and began studying as never before in her life. Hour upon hour she noted verses, looked up commentaries and compared everything with Witness literature. On the next visit she asked some tricky questions. The couple promised to answer them. Back they came, and so the discussion went on for several more visits. It ended in apparent stalemate. From that time on, no JWs have ever come back to Nancy's house!

This may seem like a pointless exercise to some. What good did it accomplish? Firstly, Nancy was built up in her own faith. She came out of the experience knowing better than ever before what she believed, and why. And because she was enabled to give a reason for the hope she had, her grasp of Christian doctrines became firmer. Nancy also developed compassion for the plight of JWs.

Secondly, the couple were challenged. Seeds of truth were planted, and as they now meet more Christians who have the grace to speak to them, those seeds will be watered. Many prayers continue for the couple, that God may grant growth. Possibly the most encouraging aspect of the whole episode was that the couple had been the object of much prayer by an ex-JW couple *before* Nancy had them directed to her doorstep! When Witnesses are contacted as a result of prayer, there is every reason to believe that God wants them reached with the truth of his love.

Reaching JWs involves a mixture of truth and love. It is useless trying one without the other, or majoring on one of them alone. The balance is a precarious one to maintain, but the effort of so doing is well worth while. It works wonders!

Because JWs believe only they have love and truth, when they see godly love displayed towards them it throws them off balance. Antagonism, ridicule, even apathy, actually reassure them, convincing them that this is evidence of the world hating them. But a mild, loving attitude does not fit in to their jigsaw-puzzle. Neither does God's truth.

In actual fact they do have a fair measure of God's truth pieced into their theological jigsaw. But because the key piece – Jesus Christ – is in the wrong place, with all the other pieces arranged accordingly, Christ's true position is not accepted. That would throw their picture of things into disarray.

Yet it should never be assumed that a reluctance to give Christ his proper place proves the Witnesses have no love of God's truth. God's Word is held in the highest esteem by the vast majority of Witnesses. This is why it is so vital to persevere in reaching them. Once they see that Jesus is the key to understanding the Bible correctly, those who do love him will be overwhelmed as the significance of his sacrificial death on the cross dawns on them.

Remember, the Governing Body has told Witnesses that it holds the key to understanding the Bible. JWs, therefore, accept its interpretation regarding the Society's supposedly theocratic (God-ruled) government and two-tier Christianity. This is entirely plausible to all but Christians who are firmly grounded in God's Word and who are 'attaining to all riches of the full assurance of understanding, to the knowledge of the mystery of God, both of the Father and of Christ, in whom are hidden all the treasures of wisdom and knowledge' (Col 2:2-3, NKJV). Paul added, 'Now this I say lest anyone should deceive you with persuasive words.' Paul could have been referring to the Watch Tower Society!

For those to whom this mystery of God remains misunderstood, it is *Christendom*, with its pathetic ignorance on the one hand and its Higher Criticism on the other, which denigrates God's Word. To be fair, the JW attitude is not entirely groundless. There is a great deal which passes as Christian which is anything but. Anyone who wants to throw mud at Christianity would never be short of sticky material. The Watch Tower Society has thrown so much mud that JWs cannot see anything else. Getting through this filthy image to the shining truth of the *real* church – the body of Christ – is a long, hard task. Every time Christendom is mentioned, Christ needs to be reintroduced into the conversation. *He* is the foundation; it is having a relationship with him that matters. When JWs point the finger at some prominent clergyman who advocates unscriptural doctrines or practices, they need to be reminded that they will not be judged on the basis of what this person has done but on their reaction to what *Jesus* has done.

This shows how vital the true gospel message is. Armageddon *may* be coming, God *may* have a millennium of peace in store, but that is not the gospel Jesus commanded his followers to preach! He said, 'This is what is written, The Christ will suffer and rise from the dead on the third day, and repentance and forgiveness of sins will be preached in his name to all nations, beginning at Jerusalem. You are witnesses to these things' (Luke 24:46-48).

The death of Christ, his resurrection, and repentance and forgiveness of sins in *his* name – that is the glorious gospel! (1 Cor 2:1-5; 15:1-4). JWs never go from house to house preaching such a message. If a Christian can do no more than emphasise the true gospel, he will have accomplished a great deal. Even a reading of Galatians 1:6-9 with its startling phrase, 'even if we or an angel from heaven should preach a gospel other than the one we preached to you, let him be eternally condemned!' could shock Witnesses into checking things out. They know their gospel places repentance and forgiveness more as an after-thought than anything else. 'Oh, yes, of course we believe faith in Jesus is vital for forgiveness,' they will say. But Witnesses do not stress it, thinking that no-one can understand the ransom doctrine until they have been taught about Armageddon and the paradise earth first. None of their books start or end with an in-depth examination of sin and the only appropriate response, which is repentance and faith in Christ.

It is vital to have clearly in mind the difference between the Society's message and the gospel, to realise how urgent the JW need is. This will serve to save the Christian from being misled and will also act as an impetus to speak directly and clearly. JWs have not yet had their sin dealt with and disposed of. They imagine that this will be a gradual process which will not be completed for at least a thousand years. The idea that their sin needs to be cancelled *now*, before they die, is nonsense because they believe that everyone who dies except Adam, Judas Iscariot, apostates etc. will be resurrected and given a second chance. Even a wayward JW who dies shortly before Armageddon will get this second chance, but those who die at a time of divine judgment such as the flood or Armageddon will never be resurrected. 'So why this peculiar sense of urgency?' they wonder. Because of attitudes like that, proclaiming the gospel to Witnesses is far from straightforward.

The fundamental truth of the gospel should never be allowed to occupy anything but first place in a Christian's dealings with Witnesses. It should be returned to, repeated and stressed to the point of boredom, if necessary. Ingenious methods of reintroducing the gospel should be invented. For instance, if a Witness starts boasting about JW neutrality in warfare, the Christian could respond, 'Ah, but the spiritual warfare currently going on is *much* more important than any visible war. I'm not neutral in *that* war. I'm a soldier of Christ, proclaiming victory and salvation only in him. Are you?' Or, if the Witness is pointing out his unique stand for God's laws, using his refusal to take blood transfusions as an example, try this line: 'How tragic that Witnesses who die refusing blood also die having refused to come under the shed blood of Christ.' Keep batting the gospel ball back into the Witness' court.

There are very many spiritual cul-de-sacs which can trap the unwary. Conscientious objection to war, refusal to take blood transfusions are but two. Any subject which leads the thoughts of Witnesses away from the person of Christ is to be avoided. It does not matter whether the Christian can prove the Witnesses wrong, even by using the Bible, because they will not be saved by debating conscientious objection or blood transfusions. Important though they are they do nothing to show Witnesses that they are heading for a lost eternity. Their sin is not addressed. In my own case, I had to realise that I was committing the sin of deliberately refusing to worship Christ. That was the 'big' sin in my life. Once I could see that, the whole matter of sin opened up to me.

As a JW I suffered from the misconception that death, being the punishment for sin, meant that everyone who died had been punished. The Day of Judgment, therefore, could make no reference to deeds committed for which punishment had already been suffered. I also believed that the small number who survived Armageddon would not need to die physically because Armageddon would be, in itself, a form of God's judgment. Therefore, those who survived this time of judgment would be deemed worthy, their past sins forgiven. This specious reasoning cannot be reconciled with the biblical doctrine about sin. One negates the other.

Only *Jesus'* death can atone for sin. Those who die physically without coming under his atonement sacrifice die spiritually too. If physical death is the sum total of punishment for sins committed whilst in the body, then there was no reason for Christ to die at Calvary! Everybody dies, therefore everybody pays for his own sins; this is the essence of JW doctrine about sin. It makes a mockery of Christ's death. But I could not understand this until the Holy Spirit began to convict me, first of my sin of deliberately refusing to worship the Saviour, then gradually of other matters. It took a long time for this issue to become clear. Indeed, I had come to grips with the doctrine of the Trinity long before I understood the atonement.

Yet my gradual awareness of the depth of the atonement was a blessing, for when the truth finally dawned on me, I was already completely assured of the Lord's love, forgiveness and acceptance of me. Did he, I wonder, realise that I had had quite enough fear to deal with in my battle from this pseudo-Christian group without the fear of damnation also being included? I know that some Christians testify to the fear of hell being a prime motivating force in their coming to Christ in repentance. It never ceases to amaze me how the Lord deals with each person as an individual. Knowing the predominant cause of our alienation from him he applies the exact remedy needed. What triggers off one person's response to him is rarely exactly the same event as another's.

But his remedy is, in one sense, always the same. He speaks the truth in love to our hearts. That is what he did with me. This is what we should always do with others.

But precisely how can we do this with JWs? It goes without saying, we need to know the truth, and have that love! We cannot impart to others what we do not have ourselves.

'Knowing the truth' is explained by Jesus who said: 'If you hold to my teaching, you are really my disciples. Then you will know the truth, and the truth will set you free' (John 8:31,32). We must remain in him, know his word, believe it and live according to it. Then not only shall *we* be set free, but we may have the blessed privilege of being used by God to set others free too.

To have godly love for others means coming into a relationship with God. Only then will we experience something of his love. Jesus said in prayer to his Father: 'I have made you known to them [the disciples], and will continue to make you known in order that the love you have for me may be in them and that I myself may be in them' (John 17:26). We must come to *know* the Father – not an intellectual knowledge, not by using 'Jehovah' as his name, for what benefit is there in calling God 'Jehovah' if we cannot call him 'Father'? To know God is to have the love of Christ enter into our hearts by the Holy Spirit's indwelling. We can know nothing of the Father until we first come to Christ (John 14:6). Through those who are in that wonderful child/Father relationship with God through Christ, his love can flow. Indeed, it *must* flow! This is the identifying mark of Christians. As John says, 'Beloved, let us love one another for love is of God; and everyone who loves is born of God and knows God' (1 John 4:7, NKJV).

Knowing Jesus is the only way to really know God (John 14:7). To know him is to come into a living relationship with a living person. JWs who accept they are not born again still claim to be in a relationship with Jesus. But how can they relate to a person to whom they refuse to talk? He is just someone they've read about. They will never see him, and they abhor prayer to him. No wonder most of their talk is about Jehovah and not Jesus and that the NWT wrongly renders John 17:3 as, 'This means everlasting life, their coming to a knowledge of you, the only true God, and the one you sent, Jesus Christ.' The Society says salvation is a head trip, taking in knowledge, learning *about* God and Jesus. That has, in their estimation to come first, because only after studying and agreeing to Society doctrines can anyone then be in a position to be baptised and become a Christian.

The correct rendering of John 17:3 is, 'Now this

is eternal life: that they may know you, the only true God, and Jesus Christ, whom you have sent.' To know God, by knowing Jesus Christ, *is* eternal life. But knowing Jesus Christ requires divine revelation as to who he is. This is a work of the Holy Spirit. When Peter confessed Jesus to be the Christ, the Son of the living God, Jesus exclaimed this was by divine revelation (Matt. 16:13-17). Spiritually dead people can *never* know who Jesus is, no matter how many books or articles they read about him. The miracle of the new birth is needed to bring the spiritually dead to life. As God said to Ezekiel, 'I will give them an undivided heart and put a new spirit in them; I will remove from them their heart of stone and give them a heart of flesh. Then they will follow my decrees and be careful to keep my laws. They will be my people, and I will be their God' (Ezek. 11:19-20). Only when a new heart is bestowed by God, can anyone then have a heart that beats for God, and a spiritual life which enacts his will.

The people of God don't have a head trip but a heart transplant. Then they begin to know God, relating to him personally, as a child relates to its parents. And they address him as 'Abba, Father.' That is what knowing God means.

Confidence

There is an immediate difference observable between those who are confident in Christ and those who are confident in themselves. The JW is confident in himself, a mature Witness having had years of training in the art of public speaking and presenting his beliefs to largely unwilling householders. He is schooled in handling objections, apathy and opposition and he has memorised an admirable number of scripture texts to which he can turn in seconds. Anyone who buys his sales pitch is then led along clear-cut lines printed in the Society's publications. All questions deemed necessary and their stated answers are already provided. Conducting a 'Bible' study is simply a matter of reading from a book. A new JW is also confident because he is accompanied by a mature Witness. If he gets into difficulties, the mature Witness will step in and help.

I started this training programme when I was just eight years old. It was called 'The Theocratic Ministry School'. There is no graduation from it. Right up till my departure from the Society some twenty years later, I was giving talks and receiving counsel. The 'Service Meeting' which followed dealt explicitly with door to door work and conducting 'Bible' studies. For two hours each week for twenty years I continued training. Added to that was a never-ending supply of books and magazines, the *Awake!* in particular providing topical subjects to facilitate conversation. To demonstrate the effect of all this 'back-up', let me share with you a recurring dream I had after leaving the Society.

I dreamt I was going from house to house, not as a JW but as a Christian. As I approached the door I felt panic rise within me; 'What will I say? How can I introduce myself?' I thought. Then my hand reached down into my bag and I pulled out *The Watchtower* and *Awake!* magazines. With relief, I knocked on the door, knowing I could start a conversation, but guilt then arose because I knew the deceptive contents of the literature I intended presenting. So I determined to simply use the magazines to start the conversation then put them back in my bag without offering them to the householder. For some years this dream plagued me. Then, one night, the victory was won. I had the same dream, but just before I knocked on the door, a thought occurred to me... in my car was my Bible. All I needed was in there! Rejoicing, I rushed down a flight of stairs, unlocked the car and picked up my Bible, throwing down the offending magazines before returning to the house. My dream ended at that point. It has never recurred since.

Those whose confidence is in God alone are conspicuously different to JWs. Their entire attitude could not be described better than by Paul's words in Romans 8:31-39:

> What, then, shall we say in response to this? If God is for us, who can be against us? He who did not spare his own Son, but gave him up for us all – how will he not also, along with him, graciously give us all things? Who will bring any charge against those whom God has chosen? It is God who justifies. Who is he that condemns? Christ Jesus, who died – more than that, who was raised to life – is at the right hand of God and is also interceding for us. Who shall separate us from the love of Christ? Shall trouble or hardship or persecution or famine or nakedness or danger or sword? As it is written: 'For your sake we face death all day long; we are considered as sheep to be slaughtered.' No, in all these things we are more than conquerors through him who loved us. For I am convinced that neither death nor life, neither angels nor demons, neither the present nor the future,

nor any powers, neither height nor depth, nor anything else in all creation, will be able to separate us from the love of God that is in Christ Jesus our Lord.

We are *more* than conquerors through him who loved us! Jesus urged his followers to take heart because he had already overcome the world (John 16:33). We, too, have overcome the world because of our faith (1 John 5:4). God leads us in triumph:

But thanks be to God, who always leads us in triumphal procession in Christ and through us spreads everywhere the fragrance of the knowledge of him. For we are to God the aroma of Christ among those who are being saved and those who are perishing. To the one we are the smell of death; to the other, the fragrance of life. And who is equal to such a task? Unlike so many, we do not peddle the word of God for profit. On the contrary, in Christ we speak before God with sincerity, like men sent from God (2 Cor 2:14-17).

Paul then goes on to show that 'the veil' is only taken away when people turn to Christ. It is the light of the gospel of the glory of Christ which is preached by Christians that results in salvation for those who are perishing. Towards the end of his letter, Paul exhorted the Corinthians saying:

The weapons we fight with are not the weapons of the world. On the contrary, they have divine power to demolish strongholds. We demolish arguments and every pretension that sets itself up against the knowledge of God, and we take captive every thought to make it obedient to Christ (2 Cor 10:4,5).

The Watch Tower Society has set itself up on high, with many arguments which act as obstacles to obeying Christ, who said no-one could come to the Father except through him. The Society declares itself to be a stronghold – a Watch Tower – into which people must flee if they are to be saved. Christians who desire to lead sincere JWs to Christ have a spiritual arsenal at their disposal with which to help set these captives free.

In the face of all this encouragement, why should any Christian feel daunted at the prospect of sharing the gospel of Christ with JWs? All he has to do is lift up Christ, by word and deed, and every false argument and pretension will be demolished. Of course he may not see any visible evidence of this triumph immediately. That is no reason to lack faith in God's promise of victory. Our task is simply stated: we tell people that concealed in Christ are all the treasures of knowledge and wisdom (Col. 2:2-4). This will prevent us from being deceived by fine-sounding arguments. It will also lift Christ up and point those who *are* deceived towards him who is the cure for this deception.

We then commend to God in prayer those to whom we have witnessed. We pray and pray and pray again, even for two long years, if necessary, as Mrs. Hodgson did for me. In the meantime, God raises up other Christians to water those seeds of truth. The fruit is his to give.

We do not fear JWs. We simply speak the truth in love to them.

Chapter 8

Being Made Perfect In Love

Being made perfect in love is an ongoing process which starts when we first begin to appreciate something of the Lord's love for us in dying at Calvary. It becomes real when we respond to that love by seeking forgiveness and Christ's salvation and continues to grow as we mature in faith. For the entire duration of our earthly walk with God, the quality of that love will improve as we humbly obey our loving Lord. Instead of hating people we once would not tolerate, we begin to feel compassion for them. Instead of being indifferent to the plight of troubled souls, we will enter into their situation in order to help ease their burdens. No longer will we shrug our shoulders at the vision of millions of people going to a lost eternity, but will cry out to God, not only for more workers to be sent into the harvest, but for God to send us to labour in these spiritual fields.

There were various JWs I could not tolerate, but after I became a Christian all my distaste for them disappeared and I started to pray earnestly for them. I actually began to feel love for them! Even when they said hurtful things about me and my new outreach work, that love remained. There was no bitterness. I realised something of the extent of God's forgiveness of me, and I simply beseeched him to be as gracious to them as he had been to me.

Looking back over the years I have been a

Christian, I can see many instances of the Lord changing my attitudes in order to change situations which seemed impossible and to reach people who seemed out of reach. Continually, my fear had to be rooted out and replaced with love. So often that fear was hidden under a blanket of worry.

The predominant worry – fear – was for my family and relatives, nearly all of whom were Witnesses. I understood only too well what my being labelled an 'apostate' meant in terms of communication with them. And it soon became clear that Christians who even mentioned my name to JWs were being avoided with almost as much repugnance as if they were 'apostates' themselves! This has even happened hundreds of miles away from where I live. How on earth would my JW relatives ever be reached with the true gospel? My anxiety led me to despair of ever seeing any of them become Christians.

One Sunday morning I went to church, as usual. But for once I was late, and not just by a few minutes either. I hesitated outside the front doors, knowing what would happen. In the Baptist church, every consideration is given to latecomers – the front pews are reserved for them! I would have to walk the length of the narrow aisle in the middle of the long hall, being scrutinised by everyone, including the pastor. I could not do it. It seemed so disrespectful to walk in late. Suddenly it occurred to me that our Pentecostal friends had a worship service, due to start in about ten minutes. Their hall was just along the next street, so I went there instead, arriving in good time.

The service started, and what a joyous way of

worshipping God they employed! Then came a time of prayer. A gentleman behind me began to pray. He said he had a word from the Lord for someone present. He began to quote Isaiah 61:3: 'To appoint unto them that mourn in Zion, to give unto them beauty for ashes, the oil of joy for mourning, the garment of praise for the spirit of heaviness; that they might be called trees of righteousness, the planting of the Lord, that he might be glorified' (KJV). As he spoke, I felt convinced that those words were for me. Do not ask me why I was so convinced. I can offer no reason. But as surely as I heard him speak, I knew I had to take that text to heart. Initially I felt puzzled. Basically my nature was a cheerful, optimistic one. I was not mournful or gloomy. What was the Lord saying to me? As the words churned around in my mind days later, they began to make sense. I was heavy of spirit because of my family. My anxiety for their eternal future was weighing heavily upon me, despairing as I was of their ever coming into covenant relationship with God. He was telling me to stop worrying – to stop being anxious. My role was to concentrate on praising him and he would take care of my family.

This notion of praising God was new to me. I had first come to grips with the concept of worshipping God, then praying to him. Now I tried to learn what praise really meant. It took some time but gradually I realised true praise was not necessarily exuberant singing, or emotionalism, but resolutely maintaining a joyful, trusting heart in the Lord even if in the midst of difficult or despairing circumstances.

This was first brought home to me after a gradual

build-up of pressure. I was increasingly involved in outreach work, and family business matters placed immense demands upon us, so much so that we had not had a holiday for three years. I knew I was tired. At first I used that fact as a reason for the gloominess I frequently felt. But the gloom deepened. I seemed to have lost my joy. That was serious enough; what was worse was the depression which I now knew was afflicting me. No longer could it be passed off as mere gloom; I recognised many of the old symptoms from my post-natal nightmare. Yet I *knew* that had been dealt with by the Lord. He had removed it completely, many years ago. It could *not* be the same depression, I told myself stubbornly. Maybe I just needed a few weeks complete rest. But no rest was in sight.

One Friday was exceptionally bad. I had a tiring day shopping and an evening bookkeeping, guaranteed in themselves to bring on depression! Late that night the telephone rang. Derek took it and said the call was for me. It was a friend whose wife was becoming a JW and whose marriage was breaking up because he was resisting all efforts to be won over. Indeed, he was objecting to the way they had changed his wife's personality and were taking control of her. I felt so depressed and did not want to take the call but I knew it must be urgent at that late hour. Stifling my anguish, I picked up the telephone. Fortunately, all I had to do was listen and promise to make a certain enquiry in the morning.

The following day I phoned an ex-JW friend who had been divorced by her Witness husband. Having dealt with the matter on hand she asked me how I was keeping. As she was a good friend I told her, unburdening myself, confessing how gripped with depression I was becoming. She listened then thoughtfully suggested that the way to stop the downward spiral of gloom was to do the very thing I seemed incapable of doing – rejoice! I needed to praise God, despite my feelings.

It was a simple solution, and the best ideas are often simple ones. I resolved to take action without delay. A few minutes later, I was walking up the lane audibly praising God, thanking him just as my friend had advised. Immediately, I felt the oppression lift like a load being shed. My lost sense of joy returned, full force. I was amazed and reminded afresh of Isaiah 61:3. It was God's doing, for there was no holiday or lessening of business pressures for two more years. Without question that had been a spiritual cure for a spiritual ailment.

The second instance of God touching me afresh with his holy joy came on the Good Friday following. It was a miserable sort of grey day right from the start. The dismal weather must have affected me for I could muster neither enthusiasm nor appetite for anything. At night I had to drive off for an errand. Heading for home, the rain pouring down, I moodily switched on the car radio. *Friday Night Is Music Night* was the programme. The compere announced the next song. It was to be a solo from Mascagni's *Cavalleria Rusticana*, the glorious Easter hymn of praise, 'O Rejoice that the Lord has arisen.'

The orchestra began to play the sublime notes and the soprano started to sing, 'O rejoice that the Lord has arisen; he has broken the gates of the prison.' As the words and music washed over me, there arose from deep within me what I can only describe as an enormous bubble of joy. It swelled with the musical crescendo till I laughed aloud in delight and joy, laughing till the tears ran down my face as bubbles of joy continued.

This was neither mirth nor hysteria. It was a brief time of deep joy which led to sober praise of God. Nobody else was present, and at no time did I lose control of myself or the car!

The Lord's touch that Good Friday was for one specific reason, that he would be honoured the next day when I provided hospitality to a JW relative and her Christian sister. Because my gloom had been eradicated with the Lord's loving prod, I was able to shake off my despondency, and praise and worship him. I could then witness to my visitors and stand back in amazement as he worked out events that day in answer to prayer. We ended up gathered around the piano singing favourite hymns! God's timing and initiative were breathtaking. If my gloominess had not been replaced with joy and praise I wonder if that day would have worked out as it did.

Assurance to keep on praying and praising
Many Christians can testify to assurance from God that he will deal with those for whom they have a particular burden. One such was Thelma Geer, a lovely elderly lady from America whom I was privileged to meet while she was visiting Scotland in 1983. Thelma had been brought up by Mormon parents and was a Mormon herself until she came to faith in Christ. Her conversion nearly broke her dear

mother's heart. Yet God assured Thelma that her mother *would* be saved. In her book, *Mormonism, Mama and Me!* Thelma wrote:

'In between God's promise to me of Mama's salvation and its fulfilment twenty years later, I was to learn the joys and duties of prayer, patience and perseverance. Those proved to be, for me, the heart of soul-winning, as well as the avenues, most times shaded and pleasant though oft-times rough and wearisome, of my daily walk with Jesus, who escorted me right up to heaven's portals the day Mama committed her soul to him' (p. 32, 3rd edition).

Perhaps the assurance was given to enable Thelma to keep praying in faith those long twenty years. What is certain is that prayer *is* the heart of soul-winning. Through God's gracious answering of fervent, persistent prayer, even the staunchest Mormon or JW can be rescued from deception, which is darkness, and transferred into the kingdom of light and truth.

Powerfully effective prayer is that which is saturated in praise from a truly joyful heart, joyful despite external circumstances. Only the God-given oil of joy and garment of praise could enable praise to bubble up through the heaviness of adverse or apparently hopeless circumstances.

The difference of relationship
The events which I have shared took place during the early years following my conversion. They are but a small selection from the Lord's activity. The point of relating them is to convey the difference in a

person's life when Jesus takes central place.

In recent years I had the joy of seeing the Lord do his transforming work of grace in the life of my twin sister, Lesley. What a difference there was in her life as Jesus entered into a saving relationship with her!

While we were together for the first seventeen years of our lives we were incredibly close, as only identical twins can be. Then she married and moved to England and we had very little contact for over twenty years. She soon drifted away from her JW roots and we became almost strangers. I had a great feeling of helplessness, wanting to be close to her, but knowing we were on completely different wavelengths. When I became a Christian I began praying for her. A few years ago my letters to her intensified in quantity and spiritual content. She responded, asking questions and raising objections. Lesley also met local Christian ladies, going for a while to their Bible study group. In her own words, Christ sneaked up behind her, then gently tapped her on the shoulder.

She says her conversion 'happened' on 30 March 1996, a week before Good Friday. Significantly, she attended a Baptist church service the month before, hearing a sermon about the resurrection of Christ. She wrote to me: 'I can honestly say this is the first time I have really appreciated the significance of the death and resurrection of Jesus Christ.'

In February of that year we were corresponding about prayer. She wrote:

'My prayers are centred around a desire for God to open up my heart, my mind, my eyes and my ears to his will. Then everything else will fall into place. For all my weaknesses, in spite of my unworthiness, I believe that, through Jesus, I can be sanctified and please our heavenly Father. Can't do it on my own, of course, so I'm asking for the Holy Spirit to enter me and guide and direct me. My biggest single hang-up, however, is handing over control and submitting. It goes against the grain. So pray for me, Anne, that I might learn humility and total surrender to God's will. It's been a long time coming. I've been resisting for years. Now I capitulate. I give up! And in doing so, I realise that by giving up everything, I will gain everything. Amen!'

Amen, indeed! The Lord was very much at work in her, leading to her baptism. The first time we were able to share communion together was a simply wonderful experience. Our relationship had not just been restored but lifted onto a higher plane because both of us were now in relationship with God through Christ. I could not travel south to be at her baptism but saw a video of the occasion. It was like watching an action replay of my own life eighteen years previously!

Since her conversion she has developed a desire to reach out to JWs. So effective was her testimony that after two visits local JWs blacklisted her home and have not returned! Undeterred, Lesley encouraged others in her church to become motivated to speak to Witnesses, arranging meetings for that purpose.

The second such meeting 'coincided' with a visit I made. Prior to the arranged meeting we went to the Sunday morning service. Just before it started, a young woman excitedly told us that her brother who was visiting had come to church with her. He was a JW who had not been to the Kingdom Hall for some eighteen months. After the service I spoke to him and he shared his story of becoming involved with the Society when he was seventeen and what had led to his lapse. As there was no belligerence in his manner and it seemed clear the Lord's hand was already upon him, I gave him copies of some articles I had written and invited him to come to that meeting two days later. He stayed on specially for it.

It was a remarkable meeting, for he was the sole JW amongst nine Christians. But what was even more remarkable was the delightful spirit of love shown towards this young man. Nobody argued with him or tried to criticise his faith. He felt free enough to respond with comments, objections and explanations to which everyone listened respectfully.

There was some risk attached to giving him freedom to explain JW views, but it is impossible to reach Witnesses whilst keeping them at arm's length. We have to draw close to them if they are to realise we love them and are not frightened of them.

He, in turn, listened to us, and he went away with more literature to read and surrounded with the prayers of nine concerned Christians! We expect to hear great things in the future as the Lord continues to deal with him. Without doubt our meeting was a divine appointment, with me travelling 400 miles south and he 200 miles east to meet in a church. When the Lord is at work, all distress I normally feel trying to speak to JWs is totally absent. That is exciting. Knowing the Lord is in control and that I just have to trust and obey gives incredible assurance.

While I was a JW nothing even approximating such assurance happened to me. I kept a detailed journal for two consecutive years after starting to pioneer. According to it, not once did the Lord reveal himself to me in any personal way nor did I expect him to. He was just someone I had read about in a book but would never meet or see. After all, he was remote, distant and in heaven. I would never go there to him and he would certainly never come to me. Nor would I have direct contact with him on the Day of Judgment, according to my estimation of that event. My journals reflected this lack of relationship despite my whole-souled, devoted JW activity. There was not even any record of a single answered prayer.

The fundamental reason I had no relationship with God whilst I was a JW was because I was ignoring Jesus' words in John 14:6: 'No-one comes to the Father except through me.' Until knowledge of what Christ had done resulted in my getting down on bended knees in heartfelt appreciation to adore his wonderful name, I remained alienated from both God the Father and the Lord Jesus Christ. The moment my eyes were opened to see Christ in his risen glory, the way of access into the Most Holy was opened up and God led me into his presence as one of his children.

As this was also Lesley's experience we are now far closer than ever we were before. All heaviness, mourning and ashes have indeed been replaced with joy and praise as we see the beauty of the Lord's work in our lives and the lives of others. 'Abba, Father' has become our prayer.

Chapter 9

Less of a Problem,
More a Matter of Prayer

The village of Luss sits on the shores of Loch Lomond, attracting many tourists due to its scenic setting, plus the fact that it was the location for STV's *Take The High Road*. One Saturday in late spring, we decided to drive over for the day as Derek wanted photographic reference for watercolours. As we were standing at the end of the pier, Derek taking photos, I gazed idly down the length of the pier and along the village road lined with quaint cottages. Tourists wandered leisurely up and down the road, and then I spotted two JW ladies, in a garden, talking to a householder. They must have been some 400 yards distant, but there was no mistaking them. One was talking animatedly, the other stood silently behind, briefcase in hand. I prayed. Then I said to Derek, 'It's been a long time since I last read a *Watchtower* magazine. Let me just wander up to those ladies and I'll see if I can get one.'

By the time the ladies left the cottage, I was nearby and approached them before they reached the next cottage path. My plan was not to enter into any kind of debate but simply to obtain a magazine, their names for prayer and an address to write to them.

'Hello,' I said. 'I wonder if I could buy a magazine from you?'

'Oh, we don't sell them,' one lady replied, 'but if anyone wants to make a donation, that's fine.'

Changed days. There used to be a fixed price for all Society literature though publishers sometimes sold it for less than cost. But around 1990/91 the Society stopped selling literature, accepting donations instead. Of course, the Society will not lose out because Witnesses still, in effect, pay the Society for all literature coming to each congregation. In theory each congregation gives a donation to the Society for this literature, but in practice it is the ordinary members (called 'publishers' – those who do the door-to-door work) who continue to more than subsidise the Society.[1]

This has always been the case, for prior to this change, millions of magazines were wasted annually, lying in publishers' cupboards, unsold but paid for by the publishers, yet included in the Society's impressive figures for average printing of each issue. Now the loss of money to the publishers will be far greater because more copies are likely to be accepted by the public if they are technically free and it is left to the individual to decide whether to pay a nominal amount, be generous, or take them for nothing. This means members will be far more out of pocket than before because they will need to give magazines out even if the donation is less than it cost them, whereas before they would say how much the magazines cost and many householders would use that as an excuse to decline to buy. Publishers still have monthly literature quotas to reach. The Society is only interested in knowing whether those quotas are reached. They make no enquiry about financial loss to individual publishers with a view to making up that loss.[2]

I offered what I hoped would be a suitable donation. The ladies were clearly curious at such an unprompted yet friendly approach. Conversation ensued and I explained I was on a day trip from Stirlingshire. They asked if I'd had much literature before.

'Oh, yes, but many years ago,' I replied truthfully.

'What do you think of it?' asked one.

So I told her politely. 'There's some truth in it, but other things concern me, particularly the emphasis on Armageddon. It seems to be Armageddon orientated.'

Now I confess this was a loaded comment because only three weeks earlier the massacre at Waco, Texas, had taken place. The cult, Branch Davidian sect, led by David Koresh, had come under siege by the FBI at their Mount Carmel compound in March 1993 for amassing weapons, all due to expectations of Armageddon coming. Over eighty people died. I mentioned this cult as an example of the dangers of building up expectations regarding Armageddon, adding the folly of the Watch Tower Society's prediction that Armageddon was going to come in 1975. Reaction to that was predictable.

'Oh! But we would never store weapons!' said the spokeswoman, sounding pained. 'And the Society did *not* say Armageddon would come in 1975.'

'When did you become a Witness?' I asked.

'After 1975,' she admitted, hastily adding, 'But the literature before then never actually said Armageddon would come in 1975. The Society

177

always stressed the unknown time lapse between Adam's creation and Eve's creation, making it impossible to calculate accurately the end of the sixth "day" of creation.'

'Well, I might be wrong,' I ventured, 'but I've got some pre-1975 literature which, I'm sure, says otherwise. Tell you what, I'll go home, look it out and tell you what it says, then you can let me know whether I've misunderstood or not.'

As the ladies found this suggestion agreeable I obtained the name and address of one of them and left, having promised to write to her.

By Monday morning a ten page epistle was in the post to Jean. Many pages contained quotes from pre-1975 literature and, never being one to do things by half, I went all the way back to false predictions regarding 1874, 1914 and 1925. The object of the exercise was to show this post-1975 convert the questionable track record of this Society for whom she was devoting sixty hours per month in proselytising work.

I did not expect a reply. Nor did I make any attempt to contact her again. What I do expect is that in answer to diligent prayer for these sincere ladies they may, in years to come, discover the real Jesus and commit themselves to him.

Very often JWs need to discover that they have been deceived by the Society before realising the need to double check Society explanations of scripture. Post-1975 converts have been given a distorted account of Society responsibility for the 1975 debacle. One of the magazines I obtained from Jean implied that people who stop serving Jehovah because expectations are not realised within a certain time period must have wrong, selfish motives.[3] Pre-1975 Witnesses have been constrained by fear to tone down their memories to suit Society explanations. An accumulation of pertinent Society statements about 1975 and other dates is a very useful tool to have handy.[4]

To deal with the 1975 blunder you need to understand that:

(1) JWs believe Christ's millennial rule begins *after* Armageddon;
(2) JWs believe this millennium marks the start of the seventh millennium from man's creation;
(3) This is why the Society used to write so much about calculating the end of 6,000 years from man's creation.

Therefore, if the Society says 6,000 years from man's creation ends in 1975, they are actually saying Armageddon will have ended by then. Or, to put it another way, they are saying Christ's millennial rule will have begun by then. Equally, if they say the seventh period of a thousand years of human history will begin in 1975, they are stating the same belief about Armageddon having ended by then and the millennium having started. Now judge for yourself:

'According to this trustworthy Bible chronology six thousand years from man's creation will end in 1975, and the seventh period of a thousand years of human history will begin in the fall of 1975 C.E.' (*Life*

Everlasting in Freedom of the Sons of God 1966, p.29).

At a pre-assembly JW meeting in 1966 at Scunthorpe, a Circuit Servant called Tommy Goulden held up the new *Life Everlasting* book (quoted above) and said, 'Brothers, do you want to know the date of Armageddon? It's in this book.' One JW present on that occasion says everyone had no doubt that Armageddon was being predicted for autumn 1975, that this idea originated with the Society's Governing Body, and they were declaring it in no uncertain terms.

Further proof of this is to be found in the *Awake!* magazine, 8 October 1968, p.14. In the two paragraphs above the heading *When Do 6,000 Years End?* it clearly expressed the JW belief that the sabbath-like millennium of Christ's rule would take place after the autumn of 1975.

'Just think, brothers, there are only about ninety months left before 6,000 years of man's existence on earth is completed. Do you remember what we learned at the assemblies last summer? The majority of people living today will probably be alive when Armageddon breaks out, and there are no resurrection hopes for those who are destroyed then' (*Kingdom Ministry* internal leaflet, March 1968, p.4).

In 1974 the May *Kingdom Ministry* leaflet, p.3, urged JWs to complete the Kingdom preaching 'since we have such a short time left now ... the end of this system is so very near! ... spend more time and energy in preaching during this final period before the present system ends.' The Society's heart was warmed to hear reports 'of brothers selling their homes and property and planning to finish out the rest of their days in this old system in the pioneer service. Certainly this is a fine way to spend the short time remaining before the wicked world's end.'

In 1968 the Society confidently said Eve was created within the same year that Adam was created (*The Watchtower*, 1 May 1968, p.271, section headed The Seventh Day, para 4). They added that 'this exciting fact fills Christians with anticipation' (ibid para 6). However, once 1975 arrived, the trumpet call became less distinct. In the 1 May 1975 *Watchtower*, p.285, the vice-president of the Society contradicted the 1 May 1968 *Watchtower* by saying the time gap between Adam and Eve's creation was unknown. This was an attempt to prolong Armageddon expectations for a few more years because JWs believe each 'day' of creation to be 1,000 years long. As Eve's creation marked the end of the sixth 'day', but the Bible does not specify how long Adam was without his helper, the Society tried to make mileage out of this. The absurdity of such excuses can hardly be grasped by non-JWs but can perhaps be illustrated.

Imagine Mary tells Jane that in October 2000 she will celebrate 25 years of marriage and as Jane is one of her best friends, she will be invited to a big celebration party. As the date approaches, Mary keeps referring to this exciting event, but no invitation is received by Jane. October 2000 passes and Jane phones Mary.

'Are things all right with you, Mary? You've not had a divorce or been widowed, have you?'

'Of course not! Why do you ask?'

'Well, it's just that I was awaiting an invitation to your Silver Wedding anniversary celebration but it never came.'

'Dear me, Jane! Don't read more into what I said than I actually did say! I only told you October 2000 would mark 25 years of my marriage. I never even mentioned the phrase "Silver Wedding". You surely didn't expect to be at a big party in October, did you?'

'Well, yes, actually. I bought an expensive dress and cancelled an important engagement so I could be free to attend.'

'But Jane, the invitation will come. Don't take the huff or I shall begin to think you are only my friend for wrong, selfish motives. One day soon the invitation will arrive, though I cannot say exactly when.'

'Why don't you know when the invitation will come?'

'Oh, it's a bit complicated because I can't calculate how long our engagement lasted. I'm sure it was only a few months – certainly less than a year – but now it seems to have been a bit longer. Once I've sorted it out I'll be able to calculate when my wedding took place and so the Silver Wedding invitations will then be posted.'

Jane would be entirely justified in never bothering to speak to such a friend again, and if an invitation did arrive, 25 years later, she would probably bin it.

An organisation which publicly tells millions of members to expect Christ's millennium by autumn

1975, then tells them years later that it's still imminent, and if they are disappointed then their motives must be selfish, is being as cruel and unreasonable as the fictitious Mary in our illustration.

As well as using such knowledge about 1975, another valid approach is to demonstrate the corruptions in the Society's *New World Translation* of the Bible. Few sincere Witnesses can abide this organisation once they discover it has been scholastically dishonest in producing its own version of the Bible. To misunderstand the Bible is understandable, but to mistranslate it in order to support an understanding is unforgivable. And because the mistranslations in question are almost exclusively concerned with the deity of Christ, there is great merit in tackling this vital issue. Of course, to be able to do this, you must be thoroughly acquainted with scripture and sound doctrine. But you don't have to be a Hebrew or a Greek scholar, although it helps if you are! What you do need is a copy of the Society's *Kingdom Interlinear Translation of the Greek Scriptures*, for it clearly shows the amazing differences between the literal translation of the Westcott and Hort Greek text which it replicates, and the Society's English rendering of it. Examples of this will follow.

It is worth pointing out to JWs at the outset that their NWT is falsely called 'a translation'. All the translating for the New Testament was done by Westcott and Hort. The Society has largely copied their work but taken liberties with it when Christ's deity was clearly shown. The lack of adequate Hebrew and Greek scholarship amongst the Society's

Translation Committee is something which should concern JWs.[5]

Another area of possible expose is the changed beliefs over the past hundred years. This can be done with reminders of the difference between 'the light getting brighter' and the light getting switched on and off. Many years ago the Society said:

> If we were following a man undoubtedly it would be different with us; undoubtedly one human idea would contradict another and that which was light one or two or six years ago would be regarded as darkness now. But with God there is no variableness, neither shadow of turning, and so it is with *truth*; any knowledge or light coming from God must be like its author. A new view of truth never can contradict a former truth. 'New light' never extinguishes older 'light', but adds to it. If you were lighting up a building containing seven gas jets you would not extinguish one every time you lighted another, but would add one light to another and they would be in harmony and thus give increase of light: so it is with the light of truth; the true increase is by adding to, not by substituting one for another.[6]

As some Society doctrines were debunked only to be returned to at a later date, no claim to 'increased light' could therefore legitimately be made. These were instances of taking one step forward, two back, then one forward. At best the Society can only claim to be no further forward on some of these matters than they were many years ago.[7]

One problem with entering into such an area is the likelihood of developing a point-scoring debate.

184

This is futile. Once Society error has been proved with much more important matters e.g. false prophecies and distortions to scripture, this area can be tackled and used as supplementary evidence of the Society's duplicity.

Seeds of truth

However, enthusiastic Christians will quickly become disheartened in reaching out to the JWs unless they realise many years usually pass before results are seen. They need to view each discussion as an opportunity to plant one or two seeds of truth and not to give up when nothing appears to result.

This was exemplified by a friend, Tom, who had several lengthy discussions with a JW man several years ago. Tom was as well versed in the Witness faith as any non-JW could be. He had years of experience in speaking to them, having developed a skilled ability in keeping deep debates going amicably. This particular contact ended when the JW man began to see the significance of Tom's points. Because the JW man realised the consequences of facing up to the truth explained to him, he stopped the discussions. Tom was really disappointed, feeling he had won the battles but lost the war. Or so it seemed.

Tom moved many miles away and some five years passed. Then unexpectedly I heard on the ex-JW grapevine of a recent convert from the JWs to Christianity, the man living in the area Tom came from. I wondered. So I wrote to this man and he contacted me. Yes, he remembered Tom very well indeed and Tom's witnessing had not been in vain. Those seeds of truth *had* taken root and the Lord had watered them and granted growth, in answer to on-going prayer.

It should now be clear that concerned Christians have a dual responsibility when witnessing to Witnesses. Not only do they need to know what the debate is all about, they must follow through with prayer, despite apparently negative results.

The responsibility to pray can be discharged without detailing how to pray here. Can the same be said of the actual debate? Should Christians use a script to help them through discussions or should they reply on spontaneous leading of the Spirit?

In my introduction I said that even the most carefully devised formula will not, in itself, guarantee a good response. There is no word-for-word script we can memorise and repeat verbatim. The simple reason for that is the unpredictable nature of individual JW responses to any given comment. With the best will in the world, a Christian cannot be sure his efforts to lead JWs along a certain path of reasoning will succeed. I have never yet heard of a JW sitting silently through a Christian's explanations.

Despite this, just such a detailed 'script' follows. But it is not intended to be a word-for-word teaching course. It is simply there to give the inexperienced Christian a flavour of the sort of debate which can ensue. It will show the kind of hurdles which might arise, and provide ideas as to possible ways of overcoming them. It demonstrates the level of spiritual dexterity needed to keep on course.

Those who feel a little daunted at the idea of such spiritual athletics should not worry. They need not even read that section. Whatever degree of spiritual understanding you have can be utilised by the Lord as you offer it to him. For some, a spontaneous remark will be sufficient, whilst for others engagement in in-depth discussion will be called for. In both cases, however, the main issues of the debate must be crystal clear at the outset:

(1) On the basis of their own beliefs, there can hardly by any JWs who are yet Christians.
(2) The JW gospel is a corruption of the biblical gospel.
(3) The JW Christ is not the biblical Christ.
(4) They therefore need to be exhorted to put their faith solely in Christ if they are to be saved.

With prayer, love and the leading of the Holy Spirit, any Christian can have the privilege of being used by God to help JWs.

As mentioned in previous chapters, JWs love a good debate in which they can demonstrate their wizardry in hopping along lists of proof texts. They have been trained to do this. What they have *not* been trained to do is linger long and hard over portions of scripture, soaking up the background and deliberating on the context of important verses. Christians who are thus schooled should employ this tactic and refuse to go with a hop, skip and a jump down the JW path. Whenever possible, they should resolutely lift up one section of scripture at a time and persuade the Witness to stop long enough to consider some of the many facets of that particular gem.

The value of this can be demonstrated in the use

of Romans 8:1-17 to show a Witness that he may not be a Christian. In order to do this you will need to surmount various JW obstacles which will be put in your way. If you have a goal and a strategy which anticipates these obstacles (or at least, the main ones) you will not fall at the first hurdle. Let's set up a virtual obstacle course as might arise when we begin to discuss Romans chapter 8 with JWs, and see how it can be tackled.

Read Romans 8:1-17. This passage is only partially understood by JWs. They have no problem grasping verses 15-17, appreciating the sonship of those who are anointed with the Holy Spirit. They happily agree with Christians that those who can say 'Abba, Father' are heirs with Christ and will be glorified with Christ; theirs is the heavenly calling. Such can partake of the bread and wine when commemorating Jesus' death. All this is true and provides an excellent starting point. Indeed, it is important to get the Witness to agree at the outset that those who are anointed with the Holy Spirit will go to heaven. Keep using the word 'anointed' whenever referring to those who will go to heaven. This is important. Affirm your mutual agreement on this point and then proceed to establish whether the Witness you are talking to is going to be a joint heir with Christ in heaven. The odds are overwhelmingly in favour of your Witness having to say, 'No, I do not have the heavenly calling.'

Now is the time to point out a subtle distortion of scripture in the NWT. Having read verses 15-17 and agreed about the meaning, compare verses 9-12, your Bible's rendering with the NWT. Point out that verse

9 in the NWT talks about God's spirit truly dwelling *in* the believer, and that your translation agrees. But ask why the NWT adds the phrase 'union with' at verse 10, when your Bible continues to simply say 'in'. All of a sudden, the NWT stops saying Christ is *in* the believer, implying that the Christian is 'in union with' Christ.

This is to enable JWs who are not anointed with the holy spirit to think that they are included, to a degree, in these biblical promises. The 'great crowd of other sheep' into which category your Witness would put himself, has been told by the Society that, as Christians, they 'have a measure' of the holy spirit. They believe that, by association with and obedience to the anointed class, they come under a sort of blanket protection, that the holy spirit given to the anointed 'spills over' to protect and guide them.[8]

The NWT encourages this erroneous notion by saying Christ can be 'in union with' believers and vice versa. The other sheep think *they* are 'in union with' Christ by their obedience to the anointed. Although they agree that the anointed differ from themselves because their calling is heavenly, they have a vision of the two classes somehow merging together, being one body, as it were. They insist that they, too, are led by God's spirit, that they are Christians.

They need to be directed to verse 14 which makes it clear that those who *are* led by God's Spirit are God's sons. The very next verse shows that these sons of God cry 'Abba, Father' and verse 17 concludes that such children of God are also joint heirs of Christ who will be glorified. At the outset,

189

you both agreed that only the anointed class can apply those verses to themselves, therefore anyone who does not have the heavenly calling is excluded from the category of sonship with God.

The Witness needs to have impressed upon him how misleading his NWT is. Urge him to check out the Greek in his *Interlinear*. Romans 8:9 is correctly rendered (apart from the lower case 's'), 'if God's spirit truly dwells in you.' Why then have additions been made to verses 1 and 10? The reason is obvious. Almost every time the NWT comes across the biblical teaching that Christ dwells *in* the believer, it waters this down to a mere 'union with' Christ which could mean just about anything. However, the NWT *does* teach the indwelling of the Holy Spirit (verse 9), thus giving rise to a subtle distortion in JW minds; one can have God's holy spirit without being anointed by the holy spirit. Witnesses think they are 'in union with' Christ, and are in harmony with God's spirit who leads them. A few of them, the anointed, also happen to have the heavenly calling, being indwelt by the holy spirit.

This is why it is important to keep referring to 'the anointed' when discussing those who are indwelt with the Holy Spirit. You need to show the Witness that he is not in this class, and until he is, he cannot claim to be led by God's Spirit. This notion, that the indwelling of the Holy Spirit is not necessary, and that those who are not indwelt can avail themselves of just as much of the Holy Spirit by studying diligently, is the huge deception blinding them to their need.

Whatever their calling, be it heavenly or earthly,

JWs think they are all Christians. This idea that there are two different Christian callings is false, but in order to get Witnesses to understand this you need to persevere with a correct exposition of Romans 8:1-17.

Thus far you have mimicked their technique of jumping about from verse to verse. But, having challenged the authenticity of the NWT, you should now have or make an opportunity to take command of the discussion.

Explain that if *your* translation of the Bible is used, a different teaching emerges. Ask him to go back to verse 1 and read all the way through to verse 17 in one go, without interruption, you doing the reading from your translation.

Then ask a question: 'What is the test by which we determine who are in harmony with the flesh, and who are in harmony with God's Spirit?' The answer is in verse 9 (even in the NWT!). The same answer is also in 2 Corinthians 13:5, but *your* translation, not the NWT, which again slips in 'union with'. This error is exposed in the *Interlinear*, so you can still use 2 Corinthians 13:5 with confidence but if you do this, don't get sidetracked. Return to Romans chapter 8.

The unequivocal answer is the indwelling of the Holy Spirit. Someone who 'belongs to Christ' has Christ's Spirit (which is the same as God's Spirit, but don't allow the Witness to launch into a debate on the nature of the Holy Spirit). Conversely, anyone who does *not* have Christ's Spirit does not belong to Christ and is not a Christian. The Witness you are talking to cannot call himself a Christian. A JW claiming to be anointed could, and I would never challenge that claim, though I would ask him how he could support a system of spiritual apartheid. The vital need of the Witness is to see that until he is indwelt (or anointed) with God's Holy Spirit, he cannot call himself a Christian. This is what Romans chapter 8 is all about; people who are indwelt with the Holy Spirit have no condemnation, but those who are not indwelt will die at enmity with God. Such are unable to please God and unable to call themselves Christians.

Of course, Witnesses will not accept this. They will vigorously protest that they are Christians, people who dedicated themselves to Jehovah, were baptised and who have faith in Jesus Christ. Don't be surprised at various endeavours to get on to different passages of scripture and to change the subject.

Stick with Romans 8. Remind your Witness that he agreed that those who are indwelt (or anointed) with the Holy Spirit have the heavenly calling. He correctly admitted that he does not have this calling. Insist that if the misleading additions of 'union with' in verses 1 and 10 are corrected (by omitting them), the true meaning is crystal clear. Romans 8 is not dealing with *three* categories of people; two Christian types and one un-Christian group. It shows that only those who have the Holy Spirit indwelling them can call themselves Christians. Such persons have the conviction that they are going to be joint heirs with Christ in heaven.

Obstacle no. 1
A standard JW response to this is to say that the Greek scriptures (New Testament to you and me) were written for anointed Christians, there was no 'other

sheep' class until the early 1930s. They think this explains everything. It does not, for it is based upon a warped interpretation of John 10:16. The context shows that Jesus spoke of believing Jews as 'his sheep', and that 'other sheep which are not of this [Jewish] fold' would be added. The prophecy in Isaiah 56:3-8 is worth using here because it shows that foreigners and eunuchs who joined themselves to Israel would be equally blessed; they would not be second-class citizens. Applied spiritually, the JWs would have to see that the other sheep joining the anointed (spiritual Israel) would have the same anointing and blessings from God; there would be no distinction between the two. They would become 'one flock'.[9]

The notion about the other sheep class emerged in the early 1930s and only came about because the Society decided then that entrance to heaven was limited to 144,000 persons. Had this idea not developed, JWs would not speak of another calling, another class. They never did prior to 1931 before which all Witnesses partook of the bread and wine and expected to go to heaven.

All divine revelation concluded with the canon of scripture, but every pseudo-Christian group depends on extra-scriptural 'revelation'. This is but one example.

There is a way of exposing the falsity of the earthly other sheep class only emerging after 1931 and it might be necessary to detour here before proceeding. First, it can be shown from scripture the error of taking the 144,000 in Revelation chapters 7 and 14 as a numerical limit for heavenly entrance.

The Witnesses have their own interpretation of the book of Revelation, claiming that the various seals and plagues took place in the nineteenth century, with the Watch Tower Society being in many instances God's channel of wrath. Various JW conventions are claimed to be the events of such outpourings when the Society read out and adopted resolutions against world governments and religions. They believed the great crowd class appeared after the 144,000 of Revelation 7:1-8 were 'sealed'.[10]

If it is pointed out that the 144,000 are taken from the 12 tribes of Israel, and that virtually all Witnesses who have ever claimed to be of this class are Gentiles, not Jews, the glib answer will be that the Bible is talking here about 'spiritual Jews', not physical Jews. Let that one pass.

Progress to verses 9-17. After reading them out aloud, go back to verses 9 and 15 and exclaim over the fact that a great crowd is in heaven! Now, isn't this surprising? JWs who hope to be part of this great crowd who survive the great tribulation are going to be in heaven, according to Revelation chapter 7. Yet they assure everyone that they will never be in heaven. Your Witness might chip in with the excuse that Revelation is once again 'spiritualising' matters and the great crowd is really on the earth while serving before God's throne in heaven in a *symbolic* manner. Let that one pass as well.

Point out verse 1 which shows that the sealing of the 144,000 takes place on the earth, not in heaven. So, in Revelation chapter 7 the 144,000 are on the earth while the great crowd are in heaven. Quite a role reversal! It isn't until chapter 14 that the 144,000 make it to heaven. Chapter 14:1 invites the innocent question, 'If 7:9 was a symbolic reference to heaven, surely 14:1 must *also* be symbolic? This must mean the 144,000 are not *really* in heaven at all; they're on the earth while serving before God's throne in heaven in a *symbolic manner.*'

By now the farcical nature of Society interpretation of Revelation will be obvious. Witnesses need to be reminded that literalising half a sentence in Revelation whilst spiritualising the other half will allow them to make Revelation mean anything they want it to mean.

Remind your Witness of the two 'explanations' you let pass earlier. In Revelation 7 he said the number 144,000 was literal but their being Jews was symbolic. He also said the un-numbered great crowd was literal but their standing before the throne of God was symbolic. Then in Revelation 14 this was reversed back to a literal presence in heaven for the 144,000. This inconsistency is obvious to all but themselves.

Assure him that God does not say one thing and then, a few chapters further on, say the same thing but intend the opposite meaning. God is consistent. If 144,000 in Revelation 7 is a literal number, it remains a literal number in chapter 14. If in Revelation 14 the 144,000 are literally in heaven, so are the great crowd in chapter 7. Entrance to heaven, although including this group of 144,000, is un-numbered and innumerable.

To take your argument from the realms of interpretation and logic to indisputable fact, you need only refer to a *Watchtower* article which exposes the Society's interpretation of Revelation 7:15 as a deception. It is the 15 August 1980 article entitled, 'The "Great Crowd" Renders Sacred Service Where?' Page 15 paragraph 4 states: 'In the Bible account of where Jesus Christ drove the money changers and merchantmen out of Herod's temple, the original Greek word is *naos*.' They say that *naos* refers to the outer temple. That is a seriously misleading statement. Get the JW to check in his *Interlinear* all four Gospel accounts, i.e. Matthew 21:12, Mark 11:15, Luke 19:45 and John 2:15, to see that the Greek word *hieron* is used.

Hieron means the entire temple complex, including the outer buildings and courtyards. *Naos* refers only to the central area of the temple, comprising the inner sanctuary building itself, within the Court of Priests where the Most Holy, Holy, Altar of Burnt Offering and the Molten Sea were located. Money changers and merchants were forbidden to enter those areas (See Vine's *Expository Dictionary of New Testament Words*).

In Revelation 7:15 the apostle John sees the great crowd in the *naos*, which means he did *not* see them in the Court of the Gentiles (which is outside the *naos*), as that *Watchtower* article tries to prove. John actually saw the great crowd in the inner sanctuary. John specifically states that the *naos* is in heaven; 'And the temple [*naos*] of God that is in heaven...' (Rev 11:19); 'And still another angel emerged from the temple [*naos*] that is in heaven...' (Rev 14:17).

The writer of that *Watchtower* article in question has deliberately tried to get the great crowd out of the inner sanctuary in heaven's temple and into the outer courts, thus permitting the meaning that they are worshipping God on earth, because to be in the Most Holy means to be in the presence of God.

This article completely misconstrues and muddles the meaning of those two Greek words in order to convince JWs that although Revelation says the great crowd are standing before the throne of God in heaven, they must remember that they are standing in the outer courts of the temple, not the inner sanctuary where God dwells. This is a classic demonstration of the lengths to which the Society will go to in order to blind its followers to the simple Bible truth that the great crowd worship God when they get to heaven.

If the Watch Tower Society remnant class have told their great crowd that it will never get to heaven when, in fact, the Bible says it will, surely that is a lie? Yet Revelation 14:5 says those of the 144,000 class (which would, according to the Society, include today's professed remnant class) are without falsehood in their mouths. [11]

Go back to Romans 8 and remind the Witness that he knows he does not have the heavenly calling. The apostle Paul said those who are anointed by God and sealed have the Holy Spirit in their hearts as a deposit, a guarantee that one day they will be with Christ in heavenly glory (2 Cor 1:21,22; 5:1-8). You have this assurance. Other Christians you know have this assurance. He does not. Something is wrong with his claim to be a Christian. It lacks the supporting evidence of the Holy Spirit's conviction.

He knows he's not part of the 144,000. Ask him if he's sure he's part of the great crowd. The great crowd have Jesus as their Mediator (John 10:11) and go to heaven (Rev 7:14-17). The Society has told him that Jesus is Mediator only for the 144,000. The anointed are in the New Covenant but nearly all JWs are neither in the Old nor the New Covenants. Has the Society misunderstood the matter of sonship?

Obstacle no. 2
Fewer than 1% of JWs claim to be indwelt, or anointed, with the Holy Spirit. Now is the time to examine who become sons of God. Read Romans 8:14. Your translation might say, 'For as many as are led by the Spirit of God, these are sons of God.' The NWT says, 'For all who are led by God's spirit, these are God's sons.' The phrase 'God's children' is used of these ones in verses 16 and 17. A son of God is a child of God; a child of God is a son of God. Ask why the NWT does not say, 'For the 144,000 who are led by God's Spirit, these are God's sons.' Why does it say 'all'? Could it be that when the Bible says 'all' it actually means 'all'? The Witness is unlikely to have agreed with you that the great crowd are in heaven along with the 144,000. He might well continue to insist that only 144,000 are anointed. Try introducing the phrase, 'born again'. This should not be difficult.

The expression 'born again' almost guarantees a stock response from Witnesses: 'Only the 144,000 are born again,' they insist. An article entitled 'Who Are Born Again?' concluded that if you are not one of the 144,000, you need *not* be born again.[12] *The Watchtower* of 15 February 1986, page 14, said: 'The "other sheep" do not need any such rebirth, for their goal is life everlasting in the restored earthly paradise as subjects of the Kingdom.' Also, *The Watchtower* of 1 April, 1988, page 18, said: '... a careful study of God's Word and Christ's teaching shows that only a limited number share the privilege of being born again' (namely, 144,000). The "great crowd" of true Christians today do not need to be born again, since their hope of everlasting life is earthly, not heavenly.'

Use Romans 8:14 to get him thinking about who are born again. First, ask him to turn to John 1:12,13. Explain that 'as many as' is exactly the same Greek word as 'all' in Romans 8:14. This can be checked in his *Interlinear*. So, John 1:12 could read, 'To all who received him, he gave authority to become children of God.' Likewise, Romans 8:14 could read, 'As many as are led by God's Spirit, these are God's sons.' All = as many as = an *un*limited number. If becoming a child/son of God is restricted to 144,000 people, the Bible has twice made a mistake; an extremely misleading mistake at that. Suggest that when the Bible says 'all', it means 'all'.

Go over John 1:12,13 again. Ask who have the authority to become born again. The biblical answer is all who receive Jesus and who believe in his name. Verse 13 unarguably shows this is talking about the new birth – being born again – becoming a child/son of God, a member of his family.

Ask the Witness if he has received Jesus, and if he exercises faith in his name. I haven't yet met a Witness who has said, 'No, I haven't accepted Jesus and I don't have faith in his name.'

If he says he has received Christ and believes in his name, then assure him that he has the right to become a child of God! Surely this thought excites him? Discomfort is more likely what he will be feeling. This does not square with what the Society has told him.

Ask him why he has not exercised this right. You have already disproved the Society's teaching on sonship – that option is no longer available. Enquire if he will partake of the bread and wine at the next Memorial service, now he realises he is entitled to become a child of God.

But perhaps there is *another* option to be considered. The realisation that he is not destined for heaven might be due to the fact that he hasn't received Jesus in the biblical sense, or believed in his name. Perhaps the Witness does not know what it means to 'receive' Jesus and to 'believe' in his name. Ask him what he thinks this means. Depending on his answer, you might need to explain it to him.

An excellent scripture to use is John 7:37-39 which shows that those who truly believe in Jesus receive the indwelling of the Holy Spirit! Philippians 2:9 is another good text but you will need to point out the NWT error of saying 'every *other* name'. (Italics mine). Their *Interlinear* shows the Greek does not have 'other' in the text. The Society has added this to detract from the unique importance of Jesus' name. They cannot have Jesus 'on par' with Jehovah. Jehovah's name, they say, is above the name of Jesus. This constitutes the real problem behind JWs not truly believing in Jesus' name.

Because there have been obstacles placed in the way of expounding Romans 8:1-17 and you have had to make some detours, turning to other related texts, you will need to recap, summarising and reminding the Witness of what has been discovered, particularly this last section on the three options he needs to consider. Try to conclude by returning again to Romans 8, emphasising that until he is anointed with the Holy Spirit, the only option open to him is the third one, that he still needs to accept Christ and believe in his name.

If you have arrived at this stage in your discussion and the Witness is still willing to continue, you will need to prepare for an in-depth examination of who Jesus *really* is, and this inevitably means explaining the deity of Christ. You would do well to call a halt, arranging another appointment and using the intervening time for prayer and preparation. If you feel unequal to the task, engage the assistance of a mature Christian who can do this with grace.

Discussing the deity of Christ is not easy. But it can be done and it must be done at some point if a Witness is to become a Christian. Before launching into a discussion, get down on your knees, then when you do discuss the Trinity, get back on your knees. Getting JWs to think is less of a problem, more a matter of prayer.

Chapter 10

Lovingly Expose
The Demi-god Myth

The subject of Christ's deity is awesome and we can only realise its truth by divine revelation. Of necessity, then, this little chapter is designed to do no more than encourage Christians who feel daunted at the prospect of tackling the Watch Tower Society's hostile attack on this foundational belief. Even so, it does not deal with every aspect of the debate. The idea is simply to provide examples of how a tenacious adhering to what the Bible actually says can break down individual Witness barriers of resistance.

There are two key concepts for handling this theological problem. First, never forget that the Society has relegated Christ to mere demi-god status yet they refuse to worship him to any degree so, in practice, Christ is just a creature. This is a myth. It prevents JWs from realising just who it was who died in agony in order that they could be rescued from their sin. They maintain it was a sinless creature. Christians maintain it was the Creator. 'Hands that flung stars into space, to cruel nails surrendered' goes a modern verse of praise; 'This is our God, the Servant King.' The JWs can only say, 'This is our demi-god, the Servant King'. Even so, they will not worship him.

Second, remember that at the end of the last chapter we said expounding the deity of Christ is less of a problem, more a matter of prayer. As it is the Holy Spirit's function to bring glory to Christ, we can prayerfully call upon divine help to lift the glorified Christ up and thereby expose the demi-god myth.

The problem will also be lessened if you have a clear overview of what the Trinity does and does not say. The Watch Tower Society has fallen into the trap of misunderstanding the Trinity and misrepresenting it. You will fall into the same trap unless you grasp the following two points:

(1) The Trinity states that within the one *Being* that is God there exists eternally three co-equal and co-eternal *Persons* – the Father, the Son and the Holy Spirit. We speak of one *what* (the Being of God) and three *whos* (the three divine Persons). Because the Society fails to acknowledge the difference between *being* (what makes something *what* it is; you and I are human beings whereas God is a divine being) and *person* (what makes someone *who* she is; I am a mother, you may not be even though you are also human), they think the Trinity says Jesus is the Father, when it says no such thing. So they major on showing from Scripture the distinct identities of the Son and the Father, as if that disproved the Trinity! What we need to be quick to point out to JWs is that we agree with them, that Jesus is not the Father, nor is the Father Jesus, and that their desire to argue this point only proves they do not know what the Trinity teaches.

(2) Trinitarians insist that the *one* Being of God is shared by *three* Persons. But JWs believe that God's Being is held by only *one* Person, the Father,

Jehovah. This is a typical form of Unitarianism. All JW writing on the Trinity assumes Unitarianism to be true. Many quotations are made from Unitarians which makes it seem as if the Society has much scholarly support for its claim that the Trinity is wide open to challenge. Yes, some clergymen, many liberal scholars and historians do not believe the Trinity. They usually do not believe the Bible to be the unerring Word of God either. If the Society truly believes the Bible to be the only authority and rule for Christians, why are they so keen to depend on such men for support? Should they not feel ashamed to be numbered in their midst?

Almost all groups which disagree with the Trinity suffer from one or both of these misunderstandings, so that's why it's important for Christians to come to grips with such matters. With the Witnesses, you will need to continually halt their repetitions of those two mistakes. Because you will be making a point which is completely new to them, they will not be likely to grasp it. A simple way of stopping them in their circuitous track is to say, 'Your Society seems to think the Trinity teaches $1 + 1 + 1 = 1$. That's not the case. The Trinity teaches $1 \times 1 \times 1 = 1$. Until your Society explains this teaching fairly, it's not in a position to criticise it.'[1]

Specious arguments and quotations
Before we begin a suggested strategy for dealing with the Trinity, it would be timely to warn of the extremely persuasive nature of Society arguments and quotations. They appear entirely reasonable to all but those schooled in theology. For example, the Society

has produced a magazine devoted to examining the Trinity. It is called *Should You Believe In the Trinity?* and even mature Christians who have long believed this teaching could be put in serious doubt by reading it. On the surface, the arguments and quotations presented seem weighty. It is only when careful digging is done, to unearth the sources from whence Society statements originate, that Christians can dismiss such a magazine as nothing more than a rehashing of old heresies in tattered disguise.

Space does not permit dealing with every dubious statement in this magazine. All I shall do here is take some examples of Society claims and expose them for what they are: a presentation designed to make readers think the Society is upholding truth when it is actually distorting facts to make them fit their anti-Trinitarian bias.

The Society presents an unbalanced picture of the Roman Catholic view of the Trinity. Despite the fact that Roman Catholicism has long upheld the Trinity doctrine, the Society only quotes negative statements from Catholic literature. However, on pages 3 and 30, it takes a more distorted liberty by saying, 'If the Trinity is false, it is degrading to Almighty God to call anyone his equal, and even worse to call Mary the 'Mother of God' ... Does it honor God to call anyone his equal? Does it honor him to call Mary 'the mother of God' and 'Mediatrix ... between the Creator and His creatures,' as does the *New Catholic Encyclopedia*?'

Quite apart from the misunderstanding about equality in the Godhead, notice how the Society links up the Trinity doctrine with calling Mary 'the mother of God' and Mary being a 'mediatrix'. People who do not know any better would think that Catholic teaching that Mary is God's mother and a mediatrix, was part of Trinity teaching. It isn't. The mediatrix idea is very recent compared with the era when the Trinity was gradually clarified whereas the cult of the Blessed Virgin was sanctioned in A.D. 432 with the term 'Mother of God' ratified then. But the term was intended to protect the humanity of Mary's offspring and was designed to say more about Jesus than his mother. The 'Immaculate Conception' of Mary was only declared *de fide* dogma (must be believed) in 1854, and the 'Bodily Assumption' declared *de fide* in 1950. As for claims that Mary is a 'co-redeemer' with Christ, this is not yet *de fide* dogma. Indeed, the Vatican's *Catholic News Service* is recorded as saying, 'The Pope will not solemnly proclaim Mary "Co-redemptrix" ... "Mediatrix" ... and "Advocate" ... This is crystal clear' (August 1997). Even enthusiastic Marian leaders like the Pope hesitate to embrace this new dogma because of the terrific damage it would do to ecumenical progress with Eastern Orthodox and Protestant groups. Biblical and Trinitarian Christians abhor these unscriptural ideas.

So, although it is true that the Society has not altogether misrepresented Catholicism in this particular instance, it certainly has misrepresented the Trinity doctrine.

Under the heading What The Ante-Nicene Fathers Taught, the Society purports to quote from Justin Martyr, Irenaeus, Tertullian, Hippolytus and Origen to prove that 'the Trinity was unknown throughout

Biblical times and for several centuries thereafter' (p.7). However, they do not give the sources for their partial quotations. The only reference given is a book called *The Church Of The First Three Centuries* by an Alvan Lamson who seems to support their anti-Trinitarian bias. It appears that the partial quotations from the Church Fathers come from this book.

Now, any author who wishes to be taken seriously needs to state his sources for quotations. This will enable anyone to check the sources for themselves, to see whether the quotations are accurate and in context, and to ensure the conclusions of the author quoted from are not misrepresented. Twenty-two years ago, while I was still a good JW but just beginning to see the need to double check the Society's quotations, I attempted to find this book by Alvan Lamson. The Society had made similar quotations from it in a 1978 *Watchtower* magazine but again provided no reference details. Two local libraries failed to obtain it for me. So I wrote to the Society headquarters in New York saying, 'I have experienced some difficulty in obtaining a book which was referred to in the 15 October 1978 *Watchtower* page 32, namely, *The Church Of The First Three Centuries* by Alvan Lamson, D.D.... Could you possibly give me any more information as to the publishers, year of printing, etc., and if the book is available in Britain, as I would like to read it for myself.'

Their reply came in a letter dated 22 December 1987: 'We inform you that this was published by Walker, Wise, and Company, 245 Washington Street, Boston, MA in 1860. We only have the one copy of this book and are fairly sure that it is now out of print.'

At that time I searched no further for it was clear my chance of obtaining an out of print American book on theology via local libraries was nil, and I had no access to any other libraries. I did wonder at the time why the Society had not obliged me with photocopies of the pertinent quotations as they said they had a copy of the book and knew I could not get one. I also wondered why their letter's fulsome details still did not contain page numbers from Lamson's book. If I had known then that those Church Fathers *did* believe in the deity of Christ as opposed to him having been created, I would not have stopped my search. When the Society's partial (and cobbled) quotes are compared with what the Church Fathers actually said, it becomes abundantly clear why the Society is so reticent to provide reference details.

Below is a selection of quotations. First comes one from the Society's *Trinity* magazine regarding a Church Father, followed by another quotation from that Church Father which completely contradicts the Society's claims.

'Justin Martyr, who died about 165 C.E., called the prehuman Jesus a created angel who is "other than the God who made all things". He said that Jesus was inferior to God and "never did anything except what the Creator ... willed him to do and say"' (*Trinity* Magazine, p.7).

'Although the Jews were always of the opinion that it was the Father of all who had spoken to Moses, it was in fact the Son of God ... who spoke to him ...

The Father of all has a Son, who is both the First-born Word of God and is God. What was said out of the bush to Moses, 'I am He who is, the God of Abraham and the God of Isaac and the God of Jacob and the God of your fathers," was an indication that they were Christ's own men' (*The Faith of the Early Fathers* by W A Jurgens, Vol. 1. p.63. Collegevill, MN: Liturgical Press, 1979, re. Justin Martyr).

'Irenaeus who died about 200 C.E., said that the prehuman Jesus had a separate existence from God and was inferior to him. He showed that Jesus is not equal to the "One true and only God," who is "supreme over all, and besides whom there is no other"' (*Trinity* magazine, p.7).

'He is Himself in His own right God and Lord and Eternal King and Only begotten and Incarnate Word, proclaimed as such by all the Prophets and by the Apostles and by the Spirit Himself.... The Scriptures would not have borne witness to these things concerning Him, if, like everyone else, He were mere man' (*Against Heresies* by Irenaeus, 3.10 pp.1-2, Jurgens, Vol. 1). '[The Gnostics] transfer the generation of the uttered word of men to the eternal Word of God, attributing to Him a beginning of utterance and a coming into being in a manner like to that of their own word. In what manner, then, would the Word of God – indeed, the great God Himself, since He is the Word – differ from the word of man, were He to have the same order and process of generation?' (ibid 2:13.8).

'Tertullian, who died about 230 C.E., taught the supremacy of God. He observed, "The Father is different from the Son [another], as he is greater; as he who begets is different from him who is begotten; he who sends, different from him who is sent." He also said: "There was a time when the Son was not ... Before all things, God was alone" (*Trinity* magazine, p.7).

'God alone is without sin. The only man without sin is Christ; for Christ is also God' (*The Soul* by Tertullian, 41.3, Jurgens, Vol. 1). ' "But Christ," they [the Gnostics] say, "also bore the nature of an angel." For what reason? And why did He take human nature?... Christ bore human nature in order to be man's salvation.... There was no such reason why Christ would take upon Himself angelic nature' (ibid 14.1).

'Hippolytus, who died about 235 C.E., said that God is "the one God, the first and the only One, the Maker and Lord of all," who "had nothing co-eval [of equal age] with him.... But he was One, alone by himself; who, willing it, called into being what had no being before" such as the created prehuman Jesus' (*Trinity* magazine, p.7).

'Only His Word is from Himself, and is therefore also God, becoming the substance of God' (*Refutation Of All Heresies* by Hippolytus, ibid 10.33).

'Origen, who died about 250 C.E., said that "the Father and Son are two substances ... two things as to their essence," and that "compared with the Father, [the Son] is a very small light"' (*Trinity* magazine, p.7).

'Although He was God, He took flesh; and having been made man, He remained what He was, God.... For we do not hold ... that some part of the substance of God was converted into the Son, or that the Son was procreated by the Father from nonexistent substances, that is, from a substance outside Himself, so that there was a time when He did not exist' (*Fundamental Doctrines* by Origen, ibid p.1, pref. 3-4).

This should suffice to show how dangerously misleading the Society's partial quotations are. It is no wonder they have not given sufficient reference details for readers to check. Their claims are so full of holes that the shabby camouflage they attempt to drape over the early Church Fathers' worship of Christ as God falls to shreds at the first tug. The Society must be scraping the bottom of the barrel. But they keep using such dishonest tactics because, so far, nobody has publicly challenged those sources. It will be interesting seeing whether they continue to use Lamson's book in this manner in the future.

It is worth remembering that the Society has shown itself to be in agreement with the ancient Gnostics who said Jesus was a created angel. One of the driving reasons behind formal construction of the Trinity doctrine in the first few centuries was the need to combat Gnostic (and other) heresies. Today Christians have a pressing need to uphold the Trinity doctrine in view of modern-day variations of such heresies, as with Watch Tower Society teaching.

Now we will consider one strategy which will anticipate the main JW obstacles.

Without wishing to minimise the awesomeness

of Christ's deity, I suggest one of the most direct ways of explaining it is to find the answer to the question, 'Should Christ be worshipped?' The benefit lies primarily in anticipating a major Witnesses objection to the deity of Christ. And a JW being asked this question will be only too eager to give you lots of reasons why Jesus should *not* be worshipped. This will get the discussion off to an excellent start, from his point of view. He will fire off lots of proof texts, imagining he's shooting you down in flames in the process. But in order to keep the subject controlled, you will have to exercise discipline. Have your plan handy, with a list of pertinent scriptures, and every scripture raised by the Witness which does not crop up in your list, let it pass. Such issues can be tackled another day. Any which do come up in your list acknowledge, but ask if you can come to them later, if they are raised in advance of your plan.

Getting started
Try something mildly agreeable like, 'The deity of Christ is a deep subject because while the Bible says only God is to be worshipped, if Jesus is God, then he too should be worshipped. Yet Jesus quoted Deuteronomy 10:20 to the devil: "You shall worship the Lord your God, and him only you shall serve". What do you think about that?'

You may have to listen for some time while the Witness enthuses about worship only being directed to Jehovah *through* Jesus, but certainly not *to* Jesus.

Come back to your starting point. Agree that both Jehovah and Jesus say exclusive worship goes to God alone. Bear in mind the Witness idea that Jesus is not God with a capital 'G'; he is 'a god' to the JW. He is not the Father, he is a created Son. He will talk about only the Father being worshipped, or only the Creator, or only God. You can agree that only the Creator, or only God is to be worshipped. But you cannot agree that only the Father is to be worshipped. Remember also that the name Jehovah is, to Witnesses, the exclusive name of God. It isn't to Christians, but you will mislead them if you agree that only Jehovah is to be worshipped.

Now get him thinking about the meaning of the word 'God'. Ask him how many true Gods there are. The answer has to be, one. Isaiah 42:8, 44:6, 46:5,9 and John 5:44 should be read as confirmation of this. The existence of many gods is acknowledged in scripture, but they are all *false* gods. They are always spoken of as being in opposition to the one and only true God, the Creator. Read Isaiah 45:21(b) and 22 at this point, followed with 2 Corinthians 4:3-5. Prepare the ground properly and prayerfully in order that the seed of truth about Christ's deity might germinate. The Witness needs to understand that either Christ is the one and only true God, or he is a false god. There is no middle ground in scripture.

To worship more than one God is polytheism which the entire Bible condemns. The only way Jesus could legitimately be worshipped would be if he were the *same* God as Jehovah, not a separate being with secondary divinity, as the Witnesses maintain. In theory they advocate polytheism because they say Jehovah is the Almighty God but Jesus is 'a [different] god'. In practice they don't commit polytheism because they stop short of giving Jesus any real worship! Their thinking is extremely muddled here because they have fallen between two stools. Depending on how a discussion goes, they will try to appear as if they are sitting on the 'Only Jehovah is to be Worshipped' stool, or the 'Our Honour and Respect for Christ is a Form of Worship' stool.

Ask the Witness to define what a god is – *any* god/God. In other words, what is the essence of godhood? The element you want them to identify is that of worship. Only deity receives worship. It might be helpful to use the illustration of a person locked in solitary confinement for years. Prayer might be the only form of worship available to him. And prayer is the one thing we offer to God which we would never offer to humans. We worship God by praying to him. Even false gods are worshipped through prayer. So, if Jesus is God, we would worship him and pray to him. If he is *not* God, it would be wrong to do that.

Now you are ready to tackle the first JW objection – only Jehovah is to be worshipped. Ask what he makes of Acts 7:54-60, Stephen's vision of heaven prior to being stoned to death. Read the passage. Stephen saw God and Jesus. He cried out aloud to Jesus, 'Lord Jesus, receive my spirit.' The NWT agrees with this but later, in verse 60, has Stephen say, 'Jehovah, do not charge this sin against them.' Other translations say 'Lord'. The *Interlinear* footnote refers to one manuscript which says Jehovah, and another which says Lord. The Westcott and Hort text in the *Interlinear* says Lord.

Challenge the Witness to consider what Stephen was doing in verse 59; he was *praying* to Jesus, and this despite the fact that his vision included Jehovah!

214

Why did he not confine his appeal to Jehovah? Surely that would have been the right thing to do if we are only to pray to God?

You will not find the Witness agreeing that Stephen was actually praying to Jesus. In that case, insist that when in verse 60 he addressed Jehovah, he could not have been praying to Jehovah either. The Witness cannot have it both ways. If Stephen's cry to Jehovah was a prayer, so was his cry to Jesus.

Press home the significance of praying to Jesus by turning to John 14:14. In the NIV and in the margin of the NKJV, Jesus says, 'You may ask *me* anything in my name and I will do it' (Italics mine). Here Jesus is giving his disciples permission to pray to him because he had just told them he was going to leave them and go to the Father. Under such circumstances the only way the disciples could ask Jesus anything would be via prayer. Of course, the NWT omits 'me'. But in the *Interlinear*, the Greek text clearly has 'me' in it! This goes beyond praying to Jehovah 'in Jesus' name'. This is praying to Jesus in Jesus' name!

A third scripture will not go amiss for the Witness will be most reluctant to accept what you say. First Corinthians 1:2 speaks about calling on the name of our Lord Jesus Christ. Christians in Corinth were doing this, as everywhere else, and Paul approved. Why don't JWs call upon the name of Jesus? Again, your Witness might try to detract from the clear statement of scripture, enthusing about praying in Jesus' name and revering him. Simply ask what it means to call upon the name of Jehovah, as in Romans 10:13, which quotes from Joel 2:32. Salvation results to those who call upon the name of

215

Jehovah. Jehovah is not going to save people who refuse to worship him. If you are familiar with the context, you could also show how, in verses 9-17, confessing the Lordship of Jesus brings salvation. Declaring the good news about *Jesus* – not Jehovah – enables people to have faith which leads to salvation. In the New Testament, calling upon the name of Jehovah equates with calling upon the name of Jesus.

If during this discussion the Witness raised the objection that Jesus is a created being and not the Creator, now is the time to examine this claim. If he has not mentioned this, do so yourself. Suggest finding out whether the Bible ever speaks of Jesus as being created, as having a beginning. You can claim confidently there is not one single scripture which speaks of Jesus as having been created. If not howls of protest, certainly a barrage of proof texts will result from such an adamant statement. Duck and wait.

Colossians 1:15 is a splendid place to start proving your claim, and will surely have been quoted by the Witness to say the exact opposite! The initial difficulty lies in misunderstanding the English translation of *prototokos,* 'first-born'. The NWT *Interlinear* is worth using here. Jesus is said to be the firstborn over (or of) creation.

When the English language uses the word 'born', we have only one meaning to attach to it. Birth in the physical sense immediately comes to mind, unless we are considering the new birth of John 3, in which case spiritual birth is meant, but either way, birth implies a starting point. Quite understandably, Witnesses read that Jesus is the firstborn and think,

'He was the very first of God's creation. Only Jehovah was in existence prior to that, for Jehovah has no beginning.' The logic is sound. But the understanding of New Testament Greek is not.

Point out that Greek has two words which might have been used by Paul in this passage. If he had used *protoktistos*, that would have translated 'first-created'. If he had wanted to say Jesus was a created being, he would most certainly have used that word. But he avoided it, choosing instead *prototokos*, which translates 'firstborn'. Why? Because to have said Jesus was the first-created of all creation would have been untrue! Jesus is *not* a created being. The Bible nowhere says Jesus was created. Proverbs 8:22-31 is a red herring used by Witnesses. They have to depend upon an interpretation of 'Wisdom' meaning Jesus Christ, and literalising the passage. If 'Wisdom' is Jesus Christ, who is 'Prudence' in verse 12? Proverbs 3:19 and 20 helps settle the matter of what is meant in Proverbs 8:22-31.

What then does 'firstborn' mean in scripture? It can refer to the first offspring born to humans or animals. But a vital clue as to its meaning when said of Jesus is given in Colossians 1:18. Jesus is called the beginning, the firstborn from the dead. Does this mean Jesus was the first person ever to be resurrected? Certainly not. Both the Old Testament and the New relate accounts of people being raised from the dead prior to Christ's resurrection. But Jesus' resurrection from the dead was distinct, unique and pre-eminently significant, and *this* is the meaning of firstborn. It refers to one who has pre-eminence above others. The firstborn son in scripture was 'above' all his siblings, obtaining the majority inheritance, and he would take over headship after his father's death. Jesus is above all others (except the Father and the Holy Spirit); he is God's pre-eminent one. He is unique and distinct from all creation because he was not created. Jesus is the Creator, but you still have a lot of convincing to do.

Continue in Colossians 1, showing up more JW misunderstanding. The NWT has corrupted the meaning of verses 16, 17 and 20 by adding the word 'other' five times, implying that Jesus was, himself, a created being. When scripture is not tampered with, Colossians 1:16-20 says Jesus is the Creator. So does John 1:1-3; '*All* things came into existence through him' (italics mine). Jesus is not the exception to this rule. The NWT *Interlinear* Greek text gives the correct rendering of Colossians and exposes the NWT English additions.

However, that is not the end of the matter. You will need to face up to Revelation 3:14 at some point. This appears to agree with the Witness claim that Jesus had a beginning because he was created by God and seems to contradict what you have been explaining.

The NWT says, 'These are the things that the Amen says, the faithful and true witness, the beginning of the creation by God.' There is no doubt that Jesus is 'the Amen'. On the surface, this looks like proof of Jesus having been created by God. But first have a look at other translations. The NKJV says, '...the Beginning of the creation of God'. Note 'of' instead of 'by'. We will see the significance of that later. The NIV says, '...the ruler of God's creation'. A completely different word, 'ruler', is used instead of 'beginning'. There seem to be some translation difficulties here. Let's see what they are.

First, *tou theou*, translated 'by God' in the NWT, but 'of God' in other translations. The Witness should check his *Interlinear*, for in the literal English underneath the Greek, Westcott and Hort have 'of the God', *not* 'by the God'. The genitive, *tou theou*, means 'of God' and not 'by God'. For the translation given in the NWT, the genitive would require the proposition *hupo* which does not occur in this passage. The NWT is misleading its readers by saying here that Jesus was created *by* God; when 'of God' is correct. But what is the sense of saying Jesus is the beginning of the creation of God? What difference does this make?

To get the sense of this, we need to find out what the Greek word *arche* means. It is usually translated 'beginning'. Greek scholars tell us, 'That by which anything begins to be, the origin, active cause' (Grimm-Thayer); 'Not the first of creatures as the Arians held and the Unitarians do now, but the originating source of creation through whom God works' (A T Robertson). Now it becomes clear why the NIV uses 'ruler'; the appropriate meaning of the Greek word *arche* has determined this choice. The NIV footnote says, 'Ruler'. The Greek word can mean first in point of time ('beginning') or first in rank ('ruler').'

Needless to say, the JWs will have none of that, electing to go for the first in point of time meaning and choosing to ignore their Society's misleading translation of *tou theou*. You will be unlikely to convince him of the true meaning of Revelation 3:14.

It is enough for you to have a clear understanding of what this verse means, to unapologetically state the case and not be swayed by the Witness' surface exposition. When a Witness has faced up to the Society's appalling translation tactics, this verse will be but one more evidence of its scholastic dishonesty.

If you have to tackle related issues like Revelation 3:14, do so, but make sure you come back to Colossians. There's more! Chapter 2:8 and 9 is dynamite, for here Paul uses Greek language to its utmost to declare the deity of Christ. First he warns about being deceived with regard to him. Jesus, he says, is that which God is, because God has his permanent abode in Jesus! Needless to say, the NWT tries to dilute this incredible declaration.

Paul could have chosen a particular word had he been meaning some kind of secondary divinity. He could have used *theiotes*, meaning 'that which is of God', or 'divine quality' (the phrase used in the NWT). He used it in Romans 1:20 because he did not want people thinking God was to be found in creation; God's invisible and divine qualities, yes, his creatorship and his Godship, yes, but not God in his person. That would be pantheism, one of the heresies which Paul warned against. But when Paul speaks of Jesus, he deliberately chooses a stronger word, *theotes*; that which God is.

The NWT says the divine quality 'dwells bodily' in Christ. Once more, Paul had a choice of words for 'dwell'. One Greek word, *paroikein*, suggests a temporary abode. Paul did not use it. He opted for the stronger word, *katoikein*; to make your permanent abode.

Could Paul have stated any more clearly than he did that Jesus is God? That which God is, Jesus is. He is the exact representation of God, not as a mirror reflects, but because he *is* God. No wonder Jesus did what his Father willed and spoke only his Father's words. No wonder the Jews tried to stone him to death for saying he and his Father were one. Any man saying such a thing, even a perfect man, would be blaspheming. But Jesus spoke the truth.

Who is the Creator?

Now is the time to progress to the positive biblical declaration that Jesus is the Creator. Witnesses believe Jesus was only used by Jehovah in creation. They say Jesus was present at creation, 'as a master-worker', and that Jehovah created *through* Jesus.

This notion is demolished in scripture. Start with Job 9:6-8, then move to Isaiah 44:24, but get the Witness to read from the NWT: 'I, Jehovah, am doing everything, stretching out the heavens *by myself*, laying out the earth. Who was with me?' (Italics mine.) The answer clearly implied is, 'Nobody'. To prove that, get the Witness to read Isaiah 48:12 and 13. Three Old Testament scriptures state God created *by himself.* His own arm created all things, not someone else's. Jesus is not God's right-arm-man; Jesus *is* God's right arm!

This last scripture (Isaiah 48:12,13) provides a superb opportunity to launch into the truth that Jesus is the Alpha and the Omega, as stated in Revelation, because the phrase, 'I am the first and the last' occurs here, as in Revelation. Witnesses insist only Jehovah can be called the Alpha and the Omega. This is because Revelation 1:8 and 21:6-7 identify the bearer of that title as Jehovah, the Almighty God. But in Revelation 1:17-18 and 2:8 the First and the Last says he was dead then came to life again. The Witnesses agree this means Jesus. They cannot have Jehovah dying due to their NWT rendering of Habakkuk 1:12: 'O my God, my Holy One, you do not die.' So, although they admit to Jesus being the First and the Last, they try to draw the line at him also being the Alpha and the Omega.

Revelation 22 is therefore problematic to JWs. But due to there being no inverted commas in New Testament Greek, the NWT has sequenced its own punctuation marks in Revelation 22 to imply Jehovah interjecting between the angel and Jesus speaking, to say *he*, not Jesus, is the Alpha and the Omega, the First and the Last, the Beginning and the End (verse 13). If it can be shown, and it can, that Jesus shares *all* those titles and not just that of First and Last, then your original statement that Jesus is the Creator will have been clearly proven.

You could take up the point that the bearer of all those titles says he is coming quickly. Jesus is identified as the one who is coming quickly just a few verses further on in verse 20. However, the Witness will correctly say that Jehovah is also spoken of in scripture as 'coming' (e.g. Rev. 1:8; 4:8; 22:7), and thus they are justified in attributing verses 12 and 13 to Jehovah, not Jesus. Direct them to Revelation 3:11 where Jesus is speaking, then go back to Isaiah 48:12 where Jehovah calls himself the first and the last, and remind them that Jesus is called by the same title in Revelation 1:17.

If the Witness becomes pedantic and tries to make mileage out of the lack of capital letters in Isaiah compared with capitals in Revelation, do a little elementary Greek with him. Direct him to the inside back page of his *Interlinear* where the Greek alphabet is listed. Ask him to identify where alpha and omega occur in the alphabet; alpha is the first letter and omega is the last. If Jehovah is the Alpha and the Omega, he is also the First and the Last. If Jesus is the First and the Last, he is also the Alpha and the Omega. Revelation 22:13 applies to Jesus. Only JWs have a problem with this verse because they refuse to acknowledge who Jesus really is – he is the Creator, who is worthy of our worship. It is a wonderful thing to see the dawning of this sublime truth on a searching JW. Sadly, there are other obstacles designed to prevent the percolation of this truth into JW minds.

JWs have been told that the Greek word commonly translated 'worship' can sometimes mean 'obeisance', a respectful attitude, even bowing down, but not actual worship. Guess which option the NWT goes for every time the Bible says Jesus is worshipped? In Hebrews 1:6 theirs is about the only translation which says, 'Let all the angels of God do obeisance to him'. The NEB says 'homage'. Most Bibles say, 'Let all God's angels worship him.' However, an interesting fact is that the NWT has not always said, 'obeisance'. The 1969 *Interlinear* says 'worship'. My 1970 deluxe NWT says 'worship'. Later editions were changed.

To tackle this issue, look at the Greek word in Revelation 5:14 translated 'worship' in the NWT. The exact same word occurs in Matthew 28:9, but because Jesus is the object of the worship, we read, '...did obeisance'. Yet in Revelation 5:14 'worship' is used because God is the object of this worship! This inconsistency betrays the intent of the Translation Committee; they did not intend their readers to read that Jesus receives worship. Of course, they slipped up with Revelation 5:13-14 because the worship in question is directed to both God *and* the Lamb, who share the same throne.

To persuade the Witness of this biased inconsistency, get him to look at John 9:38 in his *Interlinear*. In the Greek text, *prosekunesen* is rendered 'did obeisance' in the English column because Jesus receives this adulation. Compare this with Hebrews 11:21, where Jacob 'worshipped leaning upon the top of his staff' (NWT). *Exactly* the same Greek word is used. The context makes it clear that Jacob was not falling down prostrate as his act of worship because he was old and about to die. He could not get down on the ground to worship, so he leaned on the top of his staff and worshipped in that position. Therefore, this Greek word is not primarily concerned with the pose adopted in worship, but with the attitude of reverence involved.

This subject also lends itself to comparing angelic warnings against men prostrating themselves to angels, and apostolic warnings against men prostrating themselves to the apostles, with Jesus' acceptance of such reverence. Not once did Jesus say, 'Don't do that! I, too, am a man!' (cf. Rev 19:10; 22:8,9 and Acts 10:25,26 with Rev 1:17.) Jesus accepted such worship while he was on earth. The angels worship Christ in heaven. How much more should we Christians worship the risen, glorified Christ!

The truth will set JWs free

From the foregoing it can be seen that presenting biblical truth to JWs is a complicated business. It is not for the faint-hearted or for those who do not have a clear grasp of important Christian doctrine. Nor can I claim that the approaches detailed here end all argument. I have simply tried to demonstrate the sort of complications a Christian will encounter. The problems I have raised do not even constitute a comprehensive list. I have not even mentioned the Society's objections to Jesus calling himself the 'I Am', or how they get round Old Testament theophanies, or dismiss doubting Thomas' declaration of Jesus' deity, or try to prove that Christ is the archangel Michael, or how persuasively they major on Jesus' earthly life where he seemed to be limited and inferior to God. Christians should not be dismayed when such questions crop up. It was never going to be an easy job! But we are not there to overcome every single objection JWs raise. We are to glorify Christ resolutely.

This is why it is necessary to have a goal and a plan. If you simply launch into a debate with JWs, you are liable to go round in circles or end up travelling the path the JWs have been trained to take you down. As has been shown, you will need to make several detours to accommodate legitimate JW objections. You need to know how and when to detour without ending up on a JW diversion. You must know the real need of the Witnesses and persevere in pointing their need out. Be prepared. Do your homework. Have a plan and stick tenaciously to it. Promise the JWs you will consider matters they raised which you did not anticipate and discuss those issues another time. And, above all this, persevere in prayer.

There is no rigid formula which Christians can follow verbatim, guaranteeing success. What I have shared are a few ideas, born of experience, which God has been pleased to use and bless. Other Christians have other gems to offer, and if you wish to become involved in challenging JWs to consider biblical truth, you should get in touch with Christian groups who specialise in outreach to the cults.[2] There is much literature available from these ministries, giving in-depth coverage of even the most obscure Witness notions.[3] They also have experience of helping people who suffer broken marriages and who face court cases over child custody etc.

What I would stress again is the vital need to keep lifting up Jesus Christ to the Witnesses, presenting the truth about him. Only when people turn to Christ is 'the veil' taken away. The difficulty with getting JWs to turn to Christ is that they imagine they have already turned to him. The need is to show their Christ to be but a poor reflection of the real Christ, and that is a matter of divine revelation.

A personal and loving approach
I approach JWs on the basis of their own beliefs. As an ex-JW, that's not difficult for me to do! I know how they think and why they think what they think. I know why evidence which appears irrefutable to

Christians can be easily dismissed as of no account by JWs and what evidence startles them and gets them thinking. If this book has enabled you to grasp some of these nuances, it will have gone a long way to enabling you to explain the gospel to JWs in a meaningful way. I hope you will see the value of lovingly establishing contact based on common ground upon which you can both stand to begin with, before proceeding to show where you diverge and what results in taking the JW path to its logical conclusion. They are heading for a lost eternity. A clear vision of the Witnesses' dire need should prompt you to persist in reaching out to them and to pray for them.

I know that it is notoriously difficult to keep to one subject with Witnesses, to avoid mere point-scoring debate, but if your outreach is done for the Lord, and in love, it will be blessed. The blessing may not be apparent to you (as with Nancy), or it may be years later before you discover the results (as with Mrs. Hodgson and Tom). It may be that you can discuss biblical subjects in depth, or it may be that you simply quote one scripture or make one pertinent comment, then pray.

One of the most surprising results of simple outreach I ever heard was that of a Christian lady who had two young JW girls come to her door. The lady felt great love for the girls and said, 'You know, God really loves you – both of you', and the two girls burst into tears! Clearly, the Holy Spirit had prompted her to address a great need those girls had. They needed to know the love of God. JWs only talk about the love of God. They believe he is loving, they know the Bible shows his love in action, and they think they experience the love of God within the Society, but that experience does not begin to approach the love which overtakes people who are adopted into God's family.

True freedom

An immense release occurs when God's truth sets people free. JWs love to quote John 8:32, thinking they have God's truth and that they have been set free. In reality, what truth of God they do have is corrupted by the Society's half-truths and errors. Whatever worldly bondage they were liberated from by becoming JWs has only been exchanged for bondage to a man-made system of rules and servitude. They need to come to Christ before they can become his disciples, know the truth and be set free.

Jesus warned his enemies that they would die in their sin if they did not believe that he was the Messiah, sent by the Father. Like the JWs, the Jews were perplexed. They considered themselves to be free already. Jesus pointed out where true freedom lay, it lay in being set free from sin. It is sin which binds us to death and judgment. Fear of judgment cannot exist alongside God's perfect love (1 John 4:18).

Only liberation from sin brings the kind of freedom of which Jesus spoke. And only by abiding in Christ can we experience forgiveness of our sins and pass over from judgment to life. The very fact that virtually all JWs have not experienced forgiveness of their sin and do not know whether they will gain eternal life proves they do not know the truth which would make them free.

It is the sheer simplicity of that truth which baffles them. Liberation will occur when Jesus deals with their sin. *Then* they will know the truth which sets people free. *Then* they will know their Father has an abode for them in heaven. As sons of God, the Holy Spirit will convince them of their inheritance in Christ; not a paltry second-best physical existence, but a home in heaven where they will meet the one who died for them and be with him forever.

Not every JW you meet will be responsive to loving Christian outreach and be ready to 'let God be found true, though every man be found a liar', including men in the Watch Tower Society (Romans 3:4, NWT). But there are increasing numbers whose unease is growing as the years creep by and Armageddon still does not come, especially those who have been loyal members for twenty, thirty or more years. They don't like recycled explanations which sound all too familiar to excuses for previous mistaken beliefs. Those who are still in their first flush of loyalty need to know what this Society's track-record is. They are not going to get an entirely honest report in Society literature.

JWs have been deceived. If we have it 'in our hand' to do good to these deceived souls yet refrain from speaking and reaching out, we sin, and how can the love of God be in us? We have been given an understanding, a knowledge of him who is true, and of his Son, Jesus Christ. With this confidence, we can ask God to use us in outreach to such deceived people, that those whose hearts are sincere will be rescued from darkness and brought into his wonderful light, to be turned from the deceptive power of Satan to God, that they might receive forgiveness of sin and an inheritance alongside those who are sanctified by faith in Christ Jesus (Acts 26:18).

Whatever you do, if your words are gracious, seasoned with spiritual salt, and your manner is respectful and loving, those Witnesses you come into contact with will be helped towards seeing Jesus in a new, soul-saving way.

We do not fear Jehovah's Witnesses; we simply speak the truth in love to them.

Appendix

Summary Of Recent Changes To End-Time Teaching

October 1994 was the deadline for previous teaching, that the generation which saw 1914 would also see Armageddon, to hold good ('that generation' finally having been stretched out to eighty years maximum. See 8 April 1988 *Awake!* p. 14; *Aid to Bible Understanding* 1969 p. 641). The Society coped with this embarrassment by doing several things prior to and after 1994:

(1) Stressing a future 'Great Tribulation' which will start with the nations attacking world religion (Babylon the Great). This means previous teaching about when Babylon the Great fell can be subtly changed. Already, teaching about the Great Tribulation having started in 1914, then halted to allow the sheep and goats to be separated before it recommences with the destruction of Babylon the Great, has been abandoned.

(2) Stressing Jesus coming again, in great glory, with the angels, at the Great Tribulation. This gives the Society various options to now change previous teaching about his supposed coming, or presence, in 1914. It also puts 1914 teaching in the shade, all eyes now riveted on the future.

(3) Admitting the separating of the sheep from the goats has not yet begun. They used to say it had started after Jesus' presence in 1914. It is now future, awaiting this coming of Christ, in great glory, with the angels, at the Great Tribulation. It also means the great crowd will not know whether they have been judged to be sheep or goats till then.

(4) Saying the generation from which JWs will be saved is future, it will only be identified with hindsight (after the Great Tribulation has started) and it will only be of short duration, probably thirty-seven years. This means they have got rid of all the time restraints they previously encumbered themselves with by connecting 'that generation' to 1914.

(5) Saying the few anointed ones left when the Great Tribulation starts will be caught up to heaven at some point during the Great Tribulation, leaving the great crowd to carry on alone. Previously they insisted some of the anointed would be on earth into the start of the millennium. (F W Franz was asked in the Walsh Scottish Court case, 1954; 'Then the population of this new earth, will that consist of Jehovah's Witnesses alone?' He replied, 'Initially it will consist of Jehovah's Witnesses alone. The members of the remnant expect to survive that battle of Armageddon the same as a great crowd of other sheep. The continuance of the remnant upon the earth after the battle of Armageddon will be temporary.' Franz claimed to be one of the remnant and became President of the Society. cf. *The Watchtower* 1 July 1995 pp. 24-26.)

(6) Detracting JWs of the great crowd class by saying they can now have as much of the Holy Spirit as the anointed have, if they study hard and apply themselves obediently. Selecting some of the great crowd to hold positions of authority previously exclusive to the anointed shows they are training chosen JWs to take over when they disappear. The heavenly calling is now the only apparent difference between the anointed and the great crowd, implies the Society.

An unforeseen problem has recently developed and is probably directly linked to (6) above:

The steady decline in numbers of the anointed partaking of the emblems at the Memorial (due to their demise or 'falling away') has stopped. The number is now rising and if this trend continues, the Society will have to either say or do something to prevent this, or admit that their long-cherished unique teaching that only 144,000 people can ever be anointed is false.

In percentage terms, the increase in partakers in 1997 was so slight as to be hardly noticeable – only thirty-eight more. Yet this prompted the Society to arrange special one day meetings for all JWs on Saturday 4th and Sunday 5th April 1998, fully one week prior to their 11 April Memorial celebration. The Society was not so much taking a sledge hammer to smash a nut as acting swiftly and subtly to so control and regiment its members that matters would not get out of hand.

Busloads of JWs travelled to various city centres on either 4th or 5th April to be briefed on the forthcoming Memorial. Of significance was the fact that the meetings for 5 April were waived. But the Witnesses did not enjoy an unprecedented respite from their weekly *Watchtower* study at Kingdom Hall. The study article scheduled for Sunday 5 April was the second of two in the 15 February 1998 *Watchtower*, stressing the need for the other sheep not to partake of the bread and wine. Those weekend meetings were designed to use this article to leave all JWs with no doubt in their minds that more than 99.9% of them must not partake on 11 April. Here is a flavour of that magazine's tone:

'Beginning with Jesus, however, Jehovah's time had come to use the holy spirit to beget dedicated men and women to a heavenly inheritance. And what about our day? The same spirit is operating on Jesus' "other sheep," but it is not arousing in them the hope and desire for heavenly life' [p. 19 para 6].

'Particularly since 1931 have those with the earthly hope been associating with the Christian congregation. In that year, Jehovah enlightened the remnant of spirit-begotten Christians to see that Ezekiel chapter 9 refers to this earthly class, who are being marked for survival into God's new world. In 1932 it was concluded that such present-day sheeplike ones were prefigured by Jehu's associate Jonadab (Jehonadab) (2 Kings 10:15-17). In 1934 it was made clear that "Jonadabs" should "consecrate" or dedicate, themselves to God. In 1935 the "great multitude," or "great crowd" – formerly thought to be a secondary spiritual class that would be "companions" of the bride of Christ in heaven – was identified as other sheep having an earthly hope

(Revelation 7:4-15; 21:2,9; Psalm 45:14,15). And especially since 1935 have anointed ones been spearheading a search for upright people yearning to live forever on a paradise earth' [*Ibid* p. 20 para 8].

'Suppose an anointed one became unfaithful. Would there be a replacement? Paul indicated as much in his discussion of the symbolic olive tree (Romans 11:11-32). If a spirit-begotten one needs to be replaced, likely God would give the heavenly calling to someone whose faith had been exemplary in rendering sacred service to him for many years' [*Ibid* p. 20 para 10].

'*Jehovah imparts his holy spirit as a gift to his people*. Christians given a heavenly hope are anointed with holy spirit (1 John 2:20; 5:1-4, 18). Yet, God's servants having earthly prospects have the spirit's help and guidance.... So, then, possession of God's spirit does not mean that we necessarily have the heavenly calling' [*Ibid* p. 21 para 13].

'Only spirit-begotten Christians should partake because only they are in the new covenant and in the Kingdom covenant and have the undeniable testimony of God's holy spirit that theirs is the heavenly hope.... Former religious views, strong emotions arising from the death of a loved one, hardships now associated with earthly life, or the feeling of having received some special blessing from Jehovah might lead some to assume mistakenly that heavenly life is for them. But all of us should remember that the Scriptures do not command us to partake of Memorial emblems to show gratitude for Christ's ransom sacrifice' [*Ibid* p. 22 paras 16 & 17].

It is likely that Witnesses at those special meetings were also told to ensure that the many millions of interested contacts they brought along on 11 April be likewise instructed not to partake. For all their trouble, thirty-nine less people partook, world wide, than in 1997. One wonders how much interference in matters of personal conviction Witnesses can tolerate before realising they are being controlled, not by the Spirit of God, but by a tiny group of men who claim to have an (almost exclusive) anointing of 'holy spirit'.

The Blood Transfusion Crisis

But perhaps the greatest challenge to the Society's habit of interfering in matters of personal conviction is now being made by JWs themselves regarding the blood transfusion issue.

In the middle of 1997 there appeared on the Internet a 300 plus page report showing fundamental flaws and inconsistencies in the Society's blood policy. Remarkably, this was done and promoted by JW elders in good standing. This website is aimed at JWs and comes in seven languages. It is only because the JWs involved can maintain their anonymity on the Internet that they continue to function. In order to prevent the Society finding out who they are they have to change their website. It contains information like this.

'The purpose of this site is to provide other Jehovah's Witnesses with some very important information regarding the use of blood and blood fractions. Those in the media, legal and medical professions will also find this site helpful. This material has been prepared by the Associated Jehovah's Witnesses for Reform on Blood, some members of which are serving as Elders and Hospital Liaison Committee members in various congregations and branch facilities throughout the world.

The Watchtower Society will likely be forced to abandon its blood doctrine in the near future. This is a life and death issue for millions of Jehovah's Witnesses. We are in contact with the leadership in an attempt to mediate an end to the ban on the remaining blood products that Witnesses must presently refuse. We will post updates on this site. In the meantime, you should fully educate yourself on the issues so that you can intervene where necessary and appropriate to save lives and avoid blood guilt.'

This website and others like it are snowballing, providing constantly up-dated information. For example, the Society undertook to allow its Bulgarian members freedom from control or sanctions should they wish blood transfusions, in order to be registered with the Bulgarian government. The Government also agreed to provide for civilian service for JW conscientious objectors. This settlement was posted by the Secretary to the European Commission of Human Rights. Watch Tower watchers checked the matter out and began advising of possible perjury with the Society's application. It appears that even if the Bulgarian Witnesses can no longer be disfellowshipped for accepting blood, this privilege is unique to them. Other JWs need to know about this. They are unlikely to read as many facts on the matter in Society literature as they will find on the Internet.

Summary

In conclusion we can summarise the current state of the Watch Tower Society thus:

The Governing Body has three major issues to contend with if it is going to maintain its iron grip on members.

(1) Changing end-time beliefs without letting slip too soon that the 1914 doctrine is false.

(2) Stopping the trend of increasing Memorial partakers, otherwise their 144,000 doctrine will be exposed as erroneous.

(3) Dealing with the internal move for reform on the blood issue. Either way, whether they ignore it or respond by changing, it seems inevitable that legal floodgates will be opened against them.

All these problems could combine to effect a huge shake-up amongst JWs. But Witnesses will need to be informed about the issues before they can realise just how tenuous the Governing Body's position is. Even so, that in itself will not truly help individual JWs. As this book has striven to show, fear has such a relentless grip on them, most would still prefer to stick with an organisation that is cracking up than risk leaving it now – just in case Armageddon starts tomorrow ... or the day after. Loveless fear is the unhappy lot of many sincere but troubled JWs right now. They need to be liberated.

In view of the astounding about-turn which started around 1987 with The Worldwide Church of God (founded by Herbert Armstrong and known by its free magazine, *The Plain Truth* which was first published in 1934), it is just possible that a similar change might take place within The Watch Tower Society. Although the Worldwide Church of God changed by conforming to orthodox belief in the Trinity, and this seems out of the question with The Watch Tower Society, a change in the 1914 and 144,000 doctrines, combined with great disquiet about the blood issue, could start an internal shake-up with amazing repercussions. It could either split the Society in half or end the Governing Body's rule of spiritual apartheid. There could yet be a massive vote of 'no confidence' in the Governing Body which would then change everything else.

Whatever does or does not happen, any JW you meet needs all the love, informed understanding and support a Christian can muster. If ever there was a field, white and ready to harvest, it is the Jehovah's Witness field.

Notes

Introduction

1. *Daily Mail*, 14 July 1988

2. A JW lady wrote in an American JW outreach magazine, 'Free Minds Journal' (Sep/Oct 1996), about being disfellowshipped for communicating with ex-JWs on the Internet. Initially she had no idea it was a 'crime' to do this, and her motive was to defend the Society on doctrinal matters. When she checked the references provided by ex-JWs she found they were right. This so disturbed her, she stopped posting Email. Then some JW friends invited her to go on-line on a private JW bulletin board (bb). She had to be 'approved' for this, giving personal information then being accepted. She was advised not to post on the 'apostates' [ex-JWs] bb again. She didn't post anything but read what was on them.

Then one day she got a private Email from an ex-JW who expressed concern for her, hoping she was all right, and eventually she could resist no longer and posted a response. Soon after that she received a call from one of the JW brothers. He said they were on a three-way telephone call and that the other person had been in contact with the Presiding Overseer in her congregation. Her friends on the JW bb had copied posts from the bb and sent them to the elders in her congregation. Lengthy meetings with the JW elders ensued. She made more contact with the 'apostates' and was amazed at the unconditional love they had. Her final meeting with the elders was in December 1993, the issue, her loyalty to the organisation. They asked if she would stop speaking to 'those apostates'. She replied, 'No, I have not been given scriptural reason not to.' They said she would be disfellowshipped on the grounds of 'associating with apostates', and so she was.

Her story is by no means unique. Anyone with a computer, modem, and linked to an Internet provider can browse on the World Wide Web and see for themselves what is happening as information about the Watch Tower Society becomes common knowledge and JWs link up in response. This is happening primarily in America.

I recommend you 'visit' the American Free Minds Inc. web site at

http://www.freeminds.org

In Britain you can connect with Reachout Trust at

www.reachouttrust.org

or

quarterly@reachouttrust.org

Chapter 1

1. 'On inspecting the remnant of his anointed disciples in the year 1919 C.E., the reigning King Jesus Christ did find the appointed "slave" faithful and discreet in the feeding of his "domestics." Accordingly, he appointed this "slave" class over all his belongings' (*God's Kingdom of a Thousand Years Has Approached* 1975 p. 355).

Raymond Franz, who used to be a member of the Society's Governing Body (this alleged 'faithful and discreet slave') devoted a chapter in his book In Search of Christian Freedom (1991) to the Society's statements about itself as this 'slave'. His insights into the workings of this group are revelatory and well worth reading. In chapter five he exposes the falsity of the claim that Christ had a continuous 'slave' class down through the centuries spiritually feeding his people, culminating in the emergence of the modern 'slave' in 1919.

2. 'We should eat and digest and assimilate what is set before us, without shying away from parts of the food because it may not suit the fancy of our mental taste. The truths we are to publish are the ones provided through the

discreet-slave organization, not some personal opinions contrary to what the slave has provided as timely food. Jehovah and Christ direct and correct the slave as needed, not we as individuals. If we do not see a point at first we should keep trying to grasp it' (The Watchtower 1 February 1952 p. 79).

'Jehovah poured out his spirit upon them and assigned them the responsibility of serving as his sole visible channel, through whom alone spiritual instruction was to come. Those who recognize Jehovah's visible theocratic organization, therefore, must recognize and accept this appointment of the "faithful and discreet slave" and be submissive to it' (The Watchtower 1 October 1967 p.590).

'Make haste to identify the visible theocratic organization of God that represents his king, Jesus Christ. It is essential for life. Doing so, be complete in accepting its every aspect' (Ibid p. 591).

'God's visible organization today also receives theocratic guidance and direction. At the headquarters of Jehovah's Witnesses in Brooklyn, New York, there is a governing body of older Christian men from various parts of the earth who give the needed oversight to the worldwide activities of God's people. This governing body is made up of members of "the faithful and discreet slave." It serves as a spokesman for that faithful "slave."

The men of that governing body, like the apostles and older men in Jerusalem, have many years of experience in God's service. But they do not rely on human wisdom in making decisions. No, being governed theocratically, they follow the example of the early governing body in Jerusalem, whose decisions were based on God's Word and were made under the direction of holy spirit.'

'And there will be only one organization – God's visible organization – that will survive the fast-approaching "great tribulation." It is simply not true that all religions lead to the same goal... You must be part of Jehovah's organization, doing God's will, in order to receive his blessing of everlasting life' (*You Can Live Forever In Paradise On Earth*, 1982 pp. 195, 255).

'Publications of the Watch Tower Society reflect this blessing from Jehovah, and every year they lead thousands of people to Jehovah, the Source of spiritual enlightenment' (*The Watchtower* 15 February 1998, p.24).

3. Pursuers Proof of Douglas Walsh vs. The Right Honourable James Lathan Clyde M.P., P.C., as representing the Minister of Labour and National Service, November 1954, Cross-Examination of Hayden C. Covington [Society's lawyer] page 343. See also pages 345 & 346. For a complete copy of the trial write to The Scottish Record Office and ask for the above.

4. Former Governing Body member Raymond Franz said in his book: 'What, then, does the fictional teaching about a worldwide administrative and spiritual-food-supplying slave "class" accomplish? It provides a prime basis on which the organization's authority rests, by which a small group of men, whose number represents only one-seventh of one percent (0.0014) of the 8,800 "anointed," assumes the right to determine not only what all the "anointed," but in fact all Witnesses, will read, study, believe and practice. By its stress on a "class" it also serves to robe the real authority structure with a shroud of anonymity, giving the appearance of a wide diversity of membership and globality that is 'not of whole cloth,' simply not true. This fictional concept enables the real authority structure – the dozen or so members of the Governing Body – to ask for almost total obedience to their own directives without appearing as arrogant or self-serving' (*In Search Of Christian Freedom*, 1991 p. 163).

5. Initially, the Society said Jesus' second (invisible) presence occurred in 1874: 'That would not mean that Jesus

must be bodily present again on the earth... The Scriptural proof is that the second presence of the Lord Jesus Christ began in 1874 A.D.' (Prophecy 1929 pp. 64, 65).

'Our Lord, the appointed King, is now present, since October 1874' (Studies In The Scriptures Vol iv p. 621).

Armageddon was predicted to end in 1914: 'The "battle of the great day of God Almighty (Rev. 16:14), which will end in A.D. 1914 with the complete overthrow of earth's present rulership, is already commenced' (*The Time Is At Hand*, 1908 edition p.101).

Later editions of the above book show how this belief was changed to Armageddon starting in 1914, despite the statement below.

'Bear in mind that the end of 1914 is not the date for the beginning, but for the end of the time of trouble' (Zion's Watch Tower, 15 July 1894).

6. At one stage JWs thought the faithful and discreet slave was an individual man, namely, Charles T. Russell, the first President: 'Our reason was, we have FAITH that the Lord has returned, that HE is the CHIEF REAPER in this "Harvest," that HE has been supervising the work, for now about thirty-seven years, and that HE has placed Pastor Russell in charge of the work this side of the vail. We are glad therefore to recognize him as "that servant," spoken of by the Lord' (Convention Report 1911 Foreword).

Russell himself gives detailed arguments opposing the idea of a 'composite steward' or slave-class, and argues in support of an individual being the 'faithful and wise servant' in Zion's Watch Tower 15 April 1904 (which journal he edited and published.)

As the current belief about 'that servant' contradicts the Society's original teaching, they try to get out of this difficulty by saying: 'From this it is clearly seen that the editor and publisher of Zion's Watch Tower disavowed any claim to being individually, in his person, that "faithful and wise servant." He never did claim to be such' (God's

Kingdom Of A Thousand Years Has Approached, 1973 p. 346).

Yet in 1917 we read: 'The special messenger to the last Age of the Church was Charles T. Russell, born February 16, 1852. He has privately admitted his belief that he was chosen for his great work from before his birth' (The Finished Mystery, 1917 p. 53).

The Society also denied having published a biography of Russell: 'But, is it true that you have never published a biography of Pastor Russell? JOHN: That's right' (Jehovah's Witnesses In The Divine Purpose, 1959 p. 63).

Yet a Biography Of Pastor Russell was published in special editions of The Divine Plan Of The Ages in the years 1924, 1925, 1926 and 1927 with 'Copyright 1886 Watch Tower Bible & Tract Society' printed on the inside.

In the Society's most recent history book, it tries to get out of its less than honest handling of this embarrassment by resorting to 'the woman thou gavest me' excuse. They blame Russell's wife for first saying he was that 'slave', and for promoting the idea. They add that she later left him (they divorced) and that 'she parted from him because of her own desire for personal prominence.' It seems odd that they blame her both for promoting her husband and for leaving due to wanting her own promotion (Jehovah's Witnesses – Proclaimers Of God's Kingdom, 1993 pp142-143, 626).

For a thorough examination of the true story behind the Russell's divorce, see *Visions of Glory* by Barbara Grizzuti Harrison (Hale, London), a former HQ worker in New York.

7. An ironic expose of the ignorance of JWs when trying to deal with other peoples' beliefs was printed in Signs Magazine International Edition Issue No. 6 (undated) – a Muslim magazine geared towards promoting the Muslim faith. It reproduced a [private] letter written by a Scottish JW lady to a Muslim reader of the magazine. She had met

him while on door-to-door work, was invited inside, with her friend, and the householder said she could call on him again when she had read the Quran. In her letter she implied that she had indeed done research into the Quran, listing Muslim beliefs, asking a few questions and hoping 'with me doing this research as above, we could have another discussion.'

The magazine's comment on that letter was accurate when saying it was clear the JW lady's 'research' must have taken her no more than five minutes, and was obviously copied from a Society book, Reasoning From The Scriptures. Inaccuracies were pointed out and JWs admonished to read the Quran for themselves and not merely quote bits and pieces from their own books.

A pertinent quote appeared on the inside cover of that magazine: 'Do not read to contradict and refute, nor to believe and take it for granted, but to weigh and consider.' Excellent advice for JWs, Muslims and everybody else!

8. The Watchtower 15 June 1996 p. 3, and The Watchtower 15 August 1996 p. 21 as quoted in Notes (8) for chapter 9 of this book.

9. Yet the April 1918 Watchtower encouraged its readers to buy War Bonds! Also, around 1996 the Society changed its policy that JWs called up for conscription into military service must also refuse any alternative civilian service offered (thus ensuring a jail sentence for the JW.) Now they are allowed to do alternative service. Too bad for the hundreds of JWs currently languishing in prison for having refused to participate in both military and civilian service. My husband was detained at Her Majesty's pleasure for this very thing. Although he was offered work on a farm instead of National Service, he conformed to Society policy at that time. He didn't think it reasonable to refuse the alternative service but felt obliged to be obedient to the Society.

10. Raymond Franz has written about this in his book *Crisis Of Conscience*, 1994.

11. 'She [Christendom] has taken the lead in making others such an object of hatred. Whom? During World War I there was an international group of students of the Bible... This hated religious minority was composed of Christians known as International Bible Students... On these Bible Students Christendom concentrated her fire during World War I. She aimed at exterminating them. Her clergymen falsely accused them and prevailed upon political and judicial elements of this world to take repressive measures against them... In 1939-1945 C.E. a second world war wreaked havoc on mankind. But did the experience during World War I repeat itself with regard to the reanimated remnant of spiritual Israelites, who, since 1931, have been known as Jehovah's Witnesses? Despite the worst religious persecution during World War II, when the "wild beast that ascends out of the abyss" again made war with the remnant, the records answer No! Violent persecution did not succeed in putting to death the Kingdom witnessing carried on by the anointed remnant' (*Holy Spirit – The Force Behind The Coming New Order!*, pp. 141-142, 151).

12. See the Awake! 8 April 1987 article 'Speaking In Tongues – Is It From God?' wherein Dr Vinson Synan was misquoted to appear as if he opposes tongues when he does not. See the Awake! 8 September 1971 article, 'I Was An Aladura', The Watchtower 'Questions From Readers'" 15 July 1974 p. 447, and Awake! 8 April 1976 article, 'I Was A Faith Healer'.

13. 'So, then, not just a majority of Bible passages, but all the Scriptures are in agreement that God's spirit is, "not someone," but "something." A simple but careful reading of the Scriptures makes it clear that God's spirit is indeed

247

his invisible active force' (The Watchtower 15 July 1974 article, 'Is The Holy Spirit Really A Person?').

Chapter 2

1. 'Humans with flesh-and-blood bodies cannot live in heaven. Of the resurrection to heavenly life, the Bible says: "It is sown a physical body, it is raised up a spiritual body... flesh and blood cannot inherit God's kingdom" (1 Corinthians 15:44-50). Only spirit persons with spiritual bodies can live in heaven. Well, then, what happened to Jesus' fleshly body? Did not the disciples find his tomb empty? They did, because God removed Jesus' body. Why did God do this? It fulfilled what had been written in the Bible (Psalm 16:10; Acts 2:31). [Those verses actually prove it was Jesus' physical body which was raised!] Thus Jehovah saw fit to remove Jesus' body, even as he had done before with Moses' body... But since the apostle Thomas was able to put his hand into the hole in Jesus' side, does that not show that Jesus was raised from the dead in the same body that was nailed to the stake? No, for Jesus simply materialised or took on a fleshly body, as angels had done in the past' (*You Can Live Forever In Paradise On Earth*, 1982 pp. 144, 145. See also *Life Everlasting In Freedom Of The Sons Of God*, 1966 p105 para 48.

2. To demonstrate the error of the New World Translation of 1 Peter 3:18 ('...in the spirit' instead of '...by the Spirit') use the Greek text of the Society's Kingdom Interlinear of the Greek Scriptures to compare this text with Romans 8:9 and Revelation 1:10.

3. 'How, then, are we to understand the words of Revelation 1:7... Here the Bible speaks of seeing, not with physical eyes, but in the sense of discerning or perceiving... So the expression 'every eye will see him' means that everyone

will then understand or recognize that Christ is present' (*You Can Live Forever In Paradise On Earth*, p. 146 para 13).

'In the same way, Christ's return does not mean that he literally comes back to this earth. Rather, it means that he takes Kingdom power toward this earth and turns his attention to it. He does not need to leave his heavenly throne and actually come down to earth to do this. As we have seen in the previous chapter, Bible evidence shows that in the year 1914 C.E. God's time arrived for Christ to return and begin ruling' (Ibid, p. 147 para 16).

Chapter 3

1. I did not know then that in Britain the 1871 Pedlars Act prohibited using children under 17 to sell door to door without a local authority work permit. Perhaps the Society could insist its volunteer work-force could not be called 'pedlars' but unquestionably millions of children under 17 have sold millions of pieces of Society literature on door to door work. They may have changed to charity status in recent years but young children still appear to be used in just the same way as when I was a JW youngster.

2. My extensive preparations prompted me to write to the London branch office of the Society to ask them to clarify some disturbing information revealed in Canon J N D Kelly's book Early Christian Doctrine (4th ed. Adam & Charles Black, London). My letter was dated 22 September 1977. In part, my letter stated: 'The whole reason why I am digging into Canon Kelly's book is to prove to the lady that The Watchtower, Awake! and The New World Translation are 100% accurate and that such 'evidence' for the Trinity is unreliable and unscriptural. However, in Kelly's book, p. 228, Arius seems to expound certain beliefs which are quite unscriptural... '"The Father", Arius remarks, "remains ineffable to the Son, and the Word can

neither see nor know the Father perfectly and accurately...
Fourthly, the Son must be liable to change and even sin"...
Would it not be good for the brothers to be made aware of
this, as when arguing against the Trinity with some
scholarly person and using references to Arius in an
argument, such a person may seriously undermine the
soundness of our argument by exposing these errors of
Arius? As the book says about Arius's beliefs being
founded in Origen and going back to Platonic roots, we
know that such worldly reasoning is unsound and to be
guarded against, but when reading articles in the Awake!
on the Trinity, I did get the impression that the Society
looks on Arius as a defender and an upholder of the truth,
whereas it appears he was not wholly for the truth but
included worldly philosophy in his reasonings. If this is
so, and if I've analysed Canon Kelly's verbal profusion
correctly, (I've probably got it all wrong!) could you
confirm this to me and let me know if the Society holds
any views on Arius further to what the 8 January 1973
Awake! says.'

The Society's reply was dated 3 October 1977 and said
in part: 'In reply to the questions you have raised, we can
tell you that the only other main reference to Arius is way
back in the year 1944 in the Society's publications and
that was only superficial. This leaves us with the article
"How Christendom Became Trinitarian" in Awake! of
January 8, 1973, to which you have referred, and this does
give a fair coverage. We do not have in our library the
book to which you refer (Early Christian Doctrines) so we
cannot really comment upon it... Whatever the facts may
be, we have to bear in mind that we are referring in history
to the time when the Roman Catholic church was firmly
developing, long after the restraining influence of the
chosen apostles... Worldly philosophies and thinking must
have dominated any discussion. References to Arius and
Arianism are interesting really only in as much as they

show that the introduction of the trinity doctrine was not without strong opposition. This, in its way does weaken the trinitarian cause, but it does not imply that Arius was reasoning correctly in everything he said, or was the repository of Truth.'

Stating '...the only other main reference to Arius is way back in the year 1944' either showed lack of research or a desire to hide incriminating beliefs about Arius, for in The Watchtower 15 May 1925 he was called 'the Angel of Pergamum'. He was also mentioned favourably in The Watchtower 1 April 1919. And in *The Finished Mystery* (Karatol edition 1918) p. 64 he was listed amongst 'the seven Messengers to the Church'. (The other six? St Paul, St John, Waldo, Wycliffe, Luther and Russell!) Arius was definitely considered to be 'the repository of Truth' by the Watch Tower Society (as far as the Trinity was concerned) for about 50 years.

3. The 'slave' class has created loyalty based on fear – fear of being disloyal! The Watchtower 1 August 1981 illustrates this: 'Your attitude toward the wheatlike anointed "brothers" of Christ and the treatment you accord them [the remnant of the 144,000] will be the determining factor as to whether you go into 'everlasting cutting-off' or receive "everlasting life"... Prove yourself to be a loyal companion of the anointed "wheat" class, the "faithful and discreet slave," whom Christ has appointed to provide spiritual "food at the proper time."'

4. Dr J R Mantey (who is quoted on pp. 1158-1159 of early editions of Kingdom Interlinear) says of the NWT rendering of John 1:1; 'A shocking mistranslation. Obsolete and incorrect. It is neither scholarly nor reasonable to translate John 1:1 "The Word was a god".'

Dr Bruce M Metzger of Princeton (Professor of New Testament Language and Literature); 'A frightful mistranslation. Erroneous, pernicious, reprehensible. If the

Jehovah's Witnesses take this translation seriously, they are polytheists.'

Dr Samuel J Mikolaski of Zurich, Switzerland: 'This anarthrous construction does not mean what the indefinite article 'a' means in English. It is monstrous to translate the phrase "the Word was a god".'

Dr Walter R Martin (who did not teach Greek but had studied the language); 'The translation... "a god" instead of "God" is erroneous and unsupported by any good Greek scholarship, ancient or contemporary and is a translation rejected by all recognized scholars of the Greek language, many of whom are not even Christians, and cannot fairly be said to be biased in favour of the orthodox contention.'

Dr William Barclay of the University of Glasgow, Scotland; 'The deliberate distortion of truth by this sect is seen in their New Testament translations. John 1:1 is... a translation which is grammatically impossible... It is abundantly clear that a sect which can translate the New Testament like that is intellectually dishonest.'

Dr F F Bruce of the University of Manchester, England; 'Much is made by Arian amateur grammarians of the omission of the definite article with "God" in the phrase "And the Word was God". Such an omission is common with nouns in a predicative construction... "a god" would be totally indefensible.'

Dr Ernest C Colwell of the University of Chicago; 'A definite predicate nominative has the article when it follows the verb; it does not have the article when it precedes the verb... this statement cannot be regarded as strange in the prologue of the gospel which reaches its climax in the confession of Thomas, "My Lord and my God".'

Dr B F Westcott (whose Greek text – not the English part – is used in the Interlinear; 'The predicate [God] stands emphatically first, as in iv.24. It is necessarily without the article... No idea of inferiority of nature is suggested by the form of expression, which simply affirms the true deity of the Word... in the third clause "the Word" is declared to be "God" and so included in the unity of the Godhead.'

Dr J J Griesbach (whose Greek text – not the English part – is used in the Emphatic Diaglott – a favourite translation JWs use to support their own); 'So numerous and clear are the arguments and testimonies of Scriptures in favour of the true Deity of Christ, that I can hardly imagine how, upon the admission of the Divine authority of Scripture, and with regard to fair rules of interpretation, this doctrine can by any man be called into doubt. Especially the passage, John 1:1-3, is so clear and so superior to all exception, that by no daring efforts of either commentators or critics can it be snatched out of the hands of the defenders of the truth.'

Dr J Johnson of California State University, Long Beach; 'No justification whatsoever for translating theos en ho logos as 'the Word was a god'. There is no syntactical parallel to Acts 23:6 [as claimed by the Society in early editions of their Kingdom Interlinear] where there is a statement in indirect discourse; John 1:1 is direct... I am neither a Christian nor a trinitarian.'

Dr Johnson's last sentence is particularly significant in view of the Society's belief that 'To get an objective view of the matter [of correct translation]... it is best to use the nonsectarian and nonreligious Hebrew-English and Greek-English dictionaries, instead of those that have been produced by some religious denomination' (The Watchtower 1 August 1962, pp. 479-480). F W Franz was the only member of the New World Translation Committee to have any background in biblical languages.

5. On 30 May 1978 I again wrote to the Society, questioning more points of translation which I discovered by reading *The Myth Of God Incarnate* and then *The Truth Of God Incarnate*. It was the latter book which startled me. I detailed its arguments for the deity of Christ as found in

the use of Greek words in Colossians 2:9 and John 1:18. (See chapter 8 in this book for those points.)

The Society's reply was dated 10 August 1978. This was the only comment in answer to my queries;

'We notice your references to the two books... We ourselves have not read them here so we are not in a position to comment upon the points you have conveyed to us nor to tell you which manuscripts were referred to with regard to John 1:18.

As far as the trinity is concerned, we know it is not a Scriptural teaching and although clergymen try very hard to justify the teaching, the end result can only be a warping of the Scriptures... With regard to the argument regarding Colossians 2:9, we are enclosing a copy of a Watchtower question appearing in 1962 which really does explain this in some detail.'

The enclosed copy could only call upon Liddell and Scott's definition of the two terms in question '... in the light of ancient usages apart from the Scriptures"! This was also the article which urged obtaining nonsectarian and nonreligious sources to get an objective view.

6. *Theologisches Begriffslexikon zum Neuen Testament* 1965 Vol 2. The Society partially quoted one paragraph from page 606 (p. 80, English translation). To understand the full import of Schneider's statements, read from page 79 English translation, "5. God and Christ" to page 84, end of page.

7. Although the King James and other translations do not have 'me', the NWT is based upon the Westcott and Hort text which does have "me" in the Greek text.

8. The Society revived this unscriptural 'advice' in the 1970s in anticipation of their 1975 prediction for Armageddon. An article entitled 'Is This The Time To Have Children?' said: 'They have chosen to remain

254

childless so that they would be less encumbered to carry out the instructions of Jesus Christ to preach the good news of God's kingdom earth wide before the end of this system comes' (*Awake!* 8th November 1974). Then, at the 1987 District Assemblies a discourse was given entitled, 'Responsible Childbearing in This Time of The End.' It encouraged single persons to stay single and married couples to remain childless to better serve in the witnessing work made necessary because of the nearness of Armageddon. That November, another article called 'Unmarried But Complete For God's Service' said: 'But we must develop and control our circumstances so that the ministry is never relegated to a place that is less than central to our life' (*The Watchtower* 15th November 1987). It commended the Witnesses of the 'Jonadab' era who remained unmarried, free to pioneer or serve at Society headquarters. It did not admit to having employed the same scare tactics with the Jonadabs that it was using yet again with this new generation of Witnesses. That article and the following one, 'Singleness, a Rewarding Way of Life', quoted 1 Timothy 4:3, applying it to the Roman Catholics, a case of the pot calling the kettle black! The pressure upon young, single JWs continues today with such articles as 'Singleness – A Door to Undistracted Activity' being studied by JWs worldwide at Kingdom Hall meetings (*The Watchtower* 15th October 1996).

Chapter 4

1. See *Man's Salvation Out Of World Distress At Hand* pp. 343, 344, 350 & 329; The Watchtower 1 August 1981 p. 26; *You Can Live Forever In Paradise On Earth* 1982 p. 255. See also item (5) in the Appendix in this book.

2. The Society says, 'Jesus, no more and no less than a perfect human, became a ransom that compensated exactly for what Adam lost – the right to perfect human life on earth (*Should You Believe In The Trinity?*, p.15). Their anti-trinitarianism warps their understanding. If Christ was only human he could only regain what Adam lost, they say, and Adam never had the hope of going to heaven. So, where does this leave the 144,000? If the gift of heavenly perfection is not part of the ransom transaction, by what rights do the 144,000 get to go to heaven? This illustrates the theological muddle that results from denying the deity of Christ.

3. Nineteen translations which state that 'The Word was God':King James Version, The New International Version, Rotherham, Douay, Jerusalem Bible, American Standard Version, Revised Standard, Young's Literal Translation, The New Life Testament, New King James Version, New Translation (Darby), New American Standard Bible, The New Testament in Basic English, The New Testament in Modern Speech (Weymouth), The Berkley Version, The New Testament in Modern English, The New Testament in Modern English (Phillips), Emphatic Diaglott (text) *, Numeric English New Testament.

Five translations which emphasize the deity of Christ without using the exact phrase, 'The Word was God': An Expanded Translation (Wuest), The Amplified Bible, A Translation in the Language of The People (Williams), Living Bible, LAMSA.

* Although the Society tries to use Christadelphian Benjamin Wilson's Emphatic Diaglott as support for their rendering of John 1:1, the text clearly says, '... and the Logos was God.' The Society published this Emphatic Diaglott, also their various New World Translations, which are the only ones which outrightly refuse to equate Jesus the Word with God the Father. (See next note for comment on Johannes Greber's New Testament.)

256

4. In 1956 the Watch Tower Society was fully aware of the demonic influences behind Johannes Greber's New Testament (copyrighted in 1937). In a leading article, they warned JWs, 'Very plainly the spirits in which ex-priest Greber believes helped him in his translation.' (The Watchtower 15 February 1956 p. 111).

They based this warning on statements such as this from the introduction to Greber's New Testament:: '...on the occasion of my first experience with the world of divine spirits my attention had been called to the fact that the books of both the Old and the New Testament contained a great deal of spurious matter which had given rise to the many erroneous ideas prevailing in the Christian churches of our day. Subsequently I learned about these falsifications in detail... In the rare instances in which a text pronounced correct by the divine spirits can be found in none of the manuscripts available to-day, I have used the text as it was given to me by those spirits' (p. 15, 1937 edition).

An advertising brochure from the Johannes Greber Foundation says of Greber's translation work: 'At times he was given the correct answers in large illuminated letters and words passing before his eyes. Other times he was given the correct answers during prayer meetings. His wife, a medium of God's Spiritworld, was often instrumental in conveying the correct answers from God's Messengers to Pastor Greber.'

On 20 December 1980, the Watch Tower Society sent a letter from Brooklyn to the Johannes Greber Memorial Foundation. They said, 'Gentlemen: This is to acknowledge receipt of the two books you recently sent to us, The New Testament translated by Johannes Greber, and his book *Communication With The Spirit World of God*. We appreciate your sending these volumes to us. For some years we have been aware of the translation by Johannes Greber and have on occasion even quoted it.' (See *Thus Saith... The Governing Body Of Jehovah's Witnesses* p.56

by Randall Watters for photocopy of this letter and the advertising brochure.)

However, the Society deceitfully tried to give the impression that it was only in 1980 that they discovered the spiritistic background to Greber's translation. A reader of The Watchtower asked, 'Why, in recent years, has The Watchtower not made use of the translation by the former Catholic priest, Johannes Greber?'

The answer was, 'This translation was used occasionally in support of renderings of Matthew 27:52,53 and John 1:1, as given in the New World Translation and other authoritative Bible versions. But as indicated in a foreword to the 1980 edition of The New Testament by Johannes Greber, this translator relied on "God's Spirit World" to clarify for him how he should translate difficult passages. It is stated: 'His wife, a medium of God's Spiritworld, was often instrumental in conveying the correct answers from God's Messengers to Pastor Greber.' The Watchtower has deemed it improper to make use of a translation that has such a close rapport with spiritism.' (The Watchtower 1 April 1983 p 31.)

They made no reference to their article in the 15 February 1956 Watchtower magazine!

It is interesting to note how many un-Christian doctrines Greber held which the Society also holds:

* Jesus Christ is not God (*Communication With The Spirit World* p. 330)

* Jehovah alone is God the Father (*ibid* pp. 331, 333, 328, 302)

* Jesus Christ is a created being (*ibid* p. 301)

* Christ's body was not resurrected (*ibid* p. 385)

* The body of Jesus was dematerialised (*ibid* p. 385)

* There is no eternal hell (*ibid* p. 379)

* The Christian Church today is not preaching the gospel (*ibid* p. 426).

5. 'Only by regularly sharing in these congregation meetings can you develop the faith, appreciation and conviction that you need to gain God's approval' (*The Truth That Leads To Eternal Life* p. 138).

'A person may go further and claim that the Governing Body of Jehovah's Witnesses or other responsible brothers interfere with freedom of conscience and the individual's "right" to interpret the Scriptures. But remember Joseph's humble words: "Do not interpretations belong to God?" (Genesis 40:8) And did not Jesus foretell that in these final days an organization of anointed ones, "the faithful and discreet slave," would be entrusted with providing spiritual food at the proper time? (Matthew 24:45-47) Beware of those who try to put forward their own contrary opinions' (The Watchtower 15 March 1986 p. 17).

"Those who despise Jehovah's teaching include individuals who criticize and complain about Jehovah's clean organization and its rules for maintaining peace and good order. There is only a fine line of demarcation between such and those who are outright rebels. Korah and his supporters found that out to their complete undoing when they dared to be hasty in speaking against God's servant Moses" (The Watchtower 15 May 1984 p. 17).

Chapter 5

1. A scholarly examination of this thorny problem is to be found in *The Gentile Times Reconsidered* by Carl Olof Jonsson. Jonsson presents seven separate chronological lines of evidence to prove that Jerusalem fell to the Babylonians in 587 B.C., not 607 B.C., as the Society insists. The 607 date is crucial to the Society in their calculations which lead them to 1914 A.D. Any Witness desirous of establishing the truth about the 1914 date could do no better than to read this book. Jonsson has also demolished the Society's appeal to supposed increase in

earthquakes, wars, etc since 1914 as proof of 1914 being a crucial date in his book *Signs Of The Last Days*.

2. Studies In The Scriptures – The Battle Of Armageddon Vol 4 pp. 604-605.

3. The Society's first President, Charles Taze Russell, was entirely correct when he wrote, 'A new view of truth never can contradict a former truth. "New light" never extinguishes older "light" but adds to it' (Zion's Watch Tower February 1881 p. 188. Quoted in full in chapter 9, page 184, of this book).

4. See notes 4, 7 and 8 for Chapter 9.

5. 'The Watchtower of July 1, 1945, explained at length the Christian view regarding the sanctity of blood... That same article made it clear from the scriptures that only sacrificial use of blood has ever been approved by God, and that since the animal sacrifices offered under the Mosaic Law foreshadowed the sacrifice of Christ, disregard for the requirement that Christians "abstain from blood" would be an evidence of gross disregard for the ransom sacrifice of Jesus Christ. ... beginning in 1961 any who disregarded [this] requirement... were disfellow-shipped' (*Jehovah's Witnesses – Proclaimers Of God's Kingdom* 1993, p. 183).

'Occasionally you may hear someone question whether the Scriptural prohibition against eating blood really applies to transfusions. But what is behind their reasoning? Is it fear - fear of possibly losing one's present life or the life of a loved one?' (*The Watchtower* 15 March 1986, p 18).

Only a person with a death-wish would not be frightened at the thought of dying because of someone else's interpretation of scripture. And only a person with a heart of stone would not fear the same for a loved one.

6. An internal textbook for JW elders gave these instructions to elders: 'If the patient is faced with the blood issue, elders can do much to keep the situation calm and to reason with doctors and unbelieving relatives. On rare occasions a situation requires a 24-hour watch' (*Pay Attention To Yourselves And To The Flock*, 1991, p. 21, unit 1(b)).

7. As JWs refuse to see such videos or read any books exposing the Society, an ideal book to offer them is called *No Blood!* – a novel by David A Reed.

Raymond Franz has devoted a chapter to the issue of blood in *In Search Of Christian Freedom*, providing unique information on Society policy developments over the years.

8. President Rutherford understood the Acts 15 statement about blood correctly, as shown in The Watchtower 15 April 1909 pp. 116 & 117. He pointed out that the decree to abstain from blood and from things strangled were necessary recommendations and not law. He also said: 'These prohibitions had never come to the Gentiles, because they had never been under the Law Covenant; but so deeply rooted were the Jewish ideas on this subject that it was necessary to the peace of the church that the Gentiles should observe this matter also.'

Chapter 6

1. Very few JWs, however, will know what the Society is doing with regard to records of all who have been disfellowshipped. Here is a letter from a couple in California who received information about possible illegal records and Society involvement in Denmark:

'Just heard from our friend in Denmark that there was a burglary at the JW headquarters. Seems the thief took the files on disfellowshipped persons dating back some 40 years and handed it over to the press.

The story was covered not only in the newspapers but two TV channels as well.

These files had very intimate information - not only subjects such as who slept with who but also information on criminal acts that the JWs did not report to the police. This is against Danish law on the following points:

1. If someone is holding a file over people with personal sensitive information, it has to be approved by the government. Who slept with who falls into this category and the government would never allow the JWs to store that kind of information.

2. If an archive is stolen, the file holder must report to the people registered in it, that the information stored on them is on the free market.

3. If the archive revealed that the JWs did have information of criminal acts that they did not tell the government, this is clearly against the law.

The Danish police want to file a case against the JWs and some of the ex-JWs have already filed cases on them. Some newspapers are assuming that the JW leader, Jorgen Larsen, in Denmark might end up in jail for this.

If these files are recognized by the Danish law, all those mentioned can demand to see these files once a year. The JWs should only keep these records for five years.'

As reported in Comments From The Friends magazine, Fall 1992 issue, p. 9.

'Inside sources have informed us that at a recent Watch Tower Society elders' meeting they were told that:

- Disfellowshipping forms will no longer be used or kept at British headquarters. A letter will still be sent to the person concerned but no copy will be kept on file.

- When a Jehovah's Witness moves to another congregation his or her file will no longer be sent but just a report that will not be kept.

- All Jehovah's Witnesses will have to sign a form to say that they are happy for the recording of their hours to be kept.

It would appear from this that somewhere along the way the Watch Tower Society has been having trouble with the Data Protection Act. Time will tell if this is another problem they must yet face' (as reported in *Reachout Quarterly* winter 1998/9, p.11).

Chapter 9

1. JWs used to buy their own supplies of literature at the Kingdom Hall, paying the same for it as they would ask from householders. Special Pioneers got them much cheaper. I used to pay one penny (old money) for every magazine which, at that time, would be sold to the public for four pennies. Considering the paltry allowance Special Pioneers were given, such a subsidy was hardly generous. If the quota of 150 magazines per month was reached, an extra £1. 17s. 6d. could be pocketed. In a year that would be about £11. 5s. 0d., barely enough to cover shoe leather and bus fares used in 1,800 hours door-to-door work and related Witness activity. Then, once a year Special Pioneers received a clothing allowance for each month they attained 150 hours and 50 back-calls (return visits). They would get 30/- (£1. 10s. 0d.). So, in a good year, that would be £18 (figures for 1967). Longer serving Special Pioneers would get a little more. Combined with their meagre monthly living allowance, the Special Pioneer had to live off an annual income of about £212. A typical working wage in Scotland in 1967 was £1,560 per annum..

However, with the changeover from selling literature to accepting donations around 1991, JWs were expected to pay twice for their literature. Nearby the literature desk at the Kingdom Hall is a supposedly unrelated 'contribution' box. The JWs are expected to put a 'donation' in this box when they receive literature. When householders in turn give JWs a donation (whether they accept literature or not), the JWs are told they must put all of that donation into the contribution box as well. The November 1991 internal leaflet *Our Kingdom Ministry* had a question:

'Are we not donating twice for literature?' The Society answered: (p. 2)

'No. Donations that go into the contribution boxes for the Society's worldwide work are not only for the literature. Both publishers and sincerely interested persons in the field receive the literature without charge... Therefore, when donations are received from interested ones in the field, we should not say that the donation is "for the literature".'

Such statements, it would appear, are worded so as to avoid sales tax on any sale of literature, and to increase revenues. JWs who have more charitable views on this matter say they do not have to pay for the literature at all! They say they can get supplies free because they do not relate the donation they put into the contribution box with the literature received, due to such Society statements.

The inside of Society publications used to give a stated price for buying such literature. Since around 1991 this has been dropped and the statement, 'This is part of a worldwide Bible educational work that is supported by voluntary donations' appeared instead.

Despite all such theoretical 'free' literature, in practice the JWs are more than covering Society costs in producing its monumental printing output. Remember, too, that workers at Society printing plants are volunteers, receiving free board and lodgings and pocket money, but no wages.

The Watchtower 1 January 1997 claims a 17% increase in magazine placements worldwide.

2. In 1990 Society revenue was just over $1 billion, according to people who had access to computer-linked credit reporting services. In 1991 this increased by a quarter of a billion dollars to $1,248,000,000. Credit reporting services use these figures to show a company's credit-worthiness, and any business subscribing to such services can obtain a printout.

Since around 1991, Society headquarters refused to supply individuals with literature orders and they stopped printing in their magazines that subscription requests be sent to branch offices. No explanation seems to have been provided, but it is reasonable to consider that the amount of sales tax being avoided is a motivating factor.

An English company which deals with credit ratings provided these statistics on the British branch office of The Watch Tower Society, based on accounts for year ended August 1995 (all figures in millions of dollars):

	$M
Turnover	74.64
Profit before tax	31.73
Profit after tax	31.73
Shareholders funds	373.16
Return on share funds	8.50
Profit margin	42.51%

Total revenue has increased from $68.44m to $85.67m (includes donations of $70.41m). Excess of revenue over expenditure has fallen from $49.10m to $31.73m. The company has a net worth of $373.16m.

3. *The Watchtower*, 15 May 1993 p 8.

4. Changed predictions/statements about dates:

1874 – Christ's 2nd coming/return, start of his Kingdom rule. (See Studies in the Scriptures vol. iv, p.621, Prophecy pp.64-65 as quoted in Note 5, chap. 1; Zion's Watch Tower 15/7/1894, p.2; The Time is at Hand 1916 edition, p.2; Zion's WT 15/1/1892, pp.22-23.) **Current status – abandoned**.

1914 – Armageddon to end. (See Zion's WT 15/1/1892, pp.22-23; Zion's WT 15/7/1894 as quoted in Note 5, chap. 1; The Time is at Hand 1908 edition, p.110 and 1911 edition, p.101 as quoted in Note 5, chap. 1) **Current status – abandoned.**

1914 – Armageddon to start (See The Time is at Hand post 1908 editions, p.101; Pastor Russell's Sermons 1917, p.676). **Current status – abandoned.**

1914 – the Great Tribulation started. (See Light vol. 1, 1930, p.194) **Current status – abandoned.**

1914 – The true Church (the 'anointed') off to heaven. (See Religion 1951, p.324) **Current status – abandoned.**

1914 – Christ's 2nd coming/return, start of his Kingdom rule. (See Paradise Lost 1958, p.174; Forever in Paradise 1982, pp.147, 149; Proclaimers 1993, p.137) **Current status – tenuous.**

1918 – False Church/members to be destroyed. (See The Finished Mystery 1917 edition, p.485) **Current status – abandoned.**

1925 – The true Church taken to heaven and OT patriarchs resurrected to help usher in paradise on earth. (See Millions Now Living 1918/20 editions, pp.89-90; The Way to Paradise 1924. p.224; The New World 1942, p.104, 130;

JWs in the Divine Purpose 1959, p.252) **Current status – abandoned.**

1925 – Beth-Sarim mansion built for them to live in. (See The New World 1942, p.104; Consolation 17/5/42, p.104; Deed to Beth-Sarim as recorded in Kings County, San Diego, California. Copy provided by Bethel Ministries, PO Box 3818, Manhattan Beach, CA 90266) **Current status – denied.**

1931 – Separating of sheep from goats in progress. (See Paradise Lost 1958, p.200; B the G has Fallen 1963, p.467) **Current Status – abandoned.**

1975 – Millennium will start after Armageddon. (See Life Everlasting 1966, p.29; Kingdom Ministry March 1968, p.4; Watchtowers 1/5/68, p.271 and 1/5/75, p.285; Awake 8/10/68. p.14) **Current status – denied.**

5. Mr. William Cetnar, who worked for many years at Brooklyn Headquarters, stated that it was common knowledge at Brooklyn HQ that the original members of the NWT Committee were H N Knorr, F W Franz, A D Schroeder, G D Gangas, M G Henschel. For a number of years their names were a closely guarded secret. When F W Franz was asked in the 1954 Scottish trial why this was so, he replied that it was because they did 'not seek any glory or honour at the making of a translation'. A list of these gentlemens' Hebrew and/or Greek qualifications is much harder to obtain, perhaps because it appears F W Franz was the only person on that Committee with any knowledge of biblical languages.

6. Zion's Watch Tower February 1881, p.188.

7. *Will the men of Sodom be resurrected?* **Yes** – Wt July 1879, p.8. **No** – Wt 1 June 1952, p.338. **Yes** – Wt 1 Aug.

1965, p.479. No – Wt. 1 June 1988, p.31. Yes – Insight on Scriptures vol. 2 1988, p.985. No – Kingdom Ministry Dec. 1999, p.7.

Who are the 'superior authorities' of Romans 13? **Secular governments** – Wt Reprints p.1555. **God and Christ** – JWs in the Divine Purpose, p.91. **Secular governments** – Wt 15 May 1980, p.4.

Should JWs greet disfellowshipped persons? **No** – Organization 1972, p.172. **Yes** – Wt 1 Aug. 1974, pp.464-465. **No** – Wt 15 Sept. 1981, pp.24-26.

8. From 1935 the Society taught new converts to view themselves as a 'great crowd' which would not be justified by the Holy Spirit: 'The "great crowd" ... will not be justified or declared righteous either now or then as the 144,000 heavenly joint heirs have been justified while still in the flesh' (Life Everlasting 1966, p.391). However, around 1985 the Society began to change this long-held 'truth': '... the great crowd ... Because of their faith in the Lamb's shed blood, a degree of righteousness is credited to them ... a relatively righteous standing ... Like Abraham, they are accounted, or declared righteous as friends of God' (The Watchtower, 1 Dec 1985, p.17).

A further blurring of the distinction between the 144,000 and the great crowd developed: 'The "great crowd" [are] declared righteous as God's friends with a view to surviving the great tribulation' (The Watchtower, 15 Feb. 1995, p.11).

Then, in 1996 the Society began telling JWs that not having the anointing of the Holy Spirit was no barrier to having as much of the Holy Spirit as the anointed had! In an article called 'Do You Remember?' this question and its answer appeared: 'Do God's servants today who have the earthly hope have as much of God's spirit as do spirit-anointed Christians?' [Answer] 'Fundamentally, the answer is yes. God's spirit is available in equal portions to both classes, and knowledge and understanding are equally attainable by both' (The Watchtower 15 Aug. 1996, p.21). It then referred readers to The Watchtower of 15 June 1996, p.3.

This is why it is becoming increasingly important to show JWs from the Bible that those who have the Holy Spirit also have the conviction that they will be with Christ in heavenly glory. The Society is working towards the heavenly calling as being the only difference between the 144,000 and the great crowd of other sheep. It finally seems to have dawned on the Society that unless a person truly has holy spirit he cannot call himself a Christian, but instead of admitting this they are telling JWs in effect, 'Yes, you've got holy spirit too and you can have just as much of it as we do if you study hard, gain lots of knowledge and obey us, but you'll never get to heaven, no matter how diligently you apply yourselves.'

9. If further scriptural evidence is needed to demolish the false JW belief that the other sheep cannot aspire to the same hope and calling as the anointed, link the prophecy in Isaiah 56:3-8 with Galatians 3:26 – 4:7 and 21-23. Galatians 3:26, like John 1:12, challenges the Witness to face up to what 'all' means. If he claims to have faith in Christ Jesus, there can be no difference between him and all other Christians. All such receive the Spirit of Christ and can say, 'Abba, Father'.

Galatians 4:21-31 is worth using in order to turn the 144,0000 belief upside down. This can be done by pointing out the significance of the quotation from Isaiah 54:1: 'Be glad, O barren woman ... Because more are the children of the desolate woman than of her who has a husband' (vs.27). This passage takes the situation of Sarah and Hagar and applies it figuratively to show that Christians are the children of promise, Abraham's seed (cf. 3:28), through Sarah. They are in the New Covenant. Those who remain under law are children of the slave woman, Hagar, they remain in the Law Covenant and will never share the inheritance of the free woman's son. This refers to the nation of Israel who rejected Christ. So spiritual Israel (Spirit-filled Christians) are to number far more than the nation of Israel. But the Society says Abraham's seed is limited to 144,000 people (Jews and non-Jews) plus Christ Jesus. So they have 'counted' this innumerable seed and limited it to 144,001! Yet the fact that Sarah's seed numbers more than Hagar's seed is ignored, indeed, denied.

10. See 'Chart of Dates' in *Babylon the Great has Fallen* 1963, p.689 and *The Watchtower* 1 June, 1996 article 'The Serpent's Seed – How Exposed?' para. 16.

With regard to interpreting Revelation, the Society published in 1930 two volumes of *Light*, which are never used nowadays. In 1963 they published *Babylon the Great* but this has now been updated in 1988 with *Revelation – Its Grand Climax At Hand!* However, the Society continues to maintain that various resolutions adopted at assemblies, and public lectures, broadcasts and distribution of pamphlets constituted fulfilment of prophecies in Revelation about the plagues from God being poured on the nations.

With regard to the 'appearing' of the great crowd of other sheep, some clarification is needed as Society literature gives two dates, namely, 1931 and 1935. As I understand it, the Society says this new class began to form from 1931 (initially called 'the Jonadab class'): 'What, then, about the "great crowd" of sheeplike persons from all parts of the world? According to the historical facts, the time of judgment for them began in the latter part of 1931, when the anointed remnant, under the name "Jehovah's witnesses", began turning their attention to these "other sheep". The effect of this proved to be just as Jesus had predicted in his prophecy on the world's end.... Matt. 25:31-33 (*Babylon the Great*, p.467).

Although this group supposedly began to form from 1931 onwards, the Society says: 'On May 31, 1935, the "great multitude" was clearly identified' (*JWs – Proclaimers of God's Kingdom*, 1993, p.166).

11. The *Babylon the Great* book says: 'As no falsehood was found in their mouths' and 'they are without blemish', it is certain that they always speak the pure truth of the good news of God's kingdom' (p.460).

Those in the Society who claim to be of the 144,000 class have grossly distorted the good news of God's kingdom by trying to debar millions of their people from becoming part of the heavenly 'Bride of Christ'. What a corruption of God's pure truth this teaching of spiritual apartheid is!

12. *Awake!* 8 February 1988, as quoted in Chapter 1, pp.20 and 21.

Chapter 10

1. Particularly helpful explanations of the Trinity can be found in the writings of James White, especially his book *The Forgotten Trinity* (Minneapolis: Bethany House Publishers, 1998). He has also written articles refuting the Watch Tower Society's anti-trinitarian arguments in the Christian Research Institute's *Journal*. One such article is a book review critique of *Jehovah's Witnesses Defended – an answer to scholars and critics* by Greg Stafford, a JW Stafford's book (*not* published by the Society) is acknowledged by White to be unusual in that 'Stafford demonstrates a familiarity with many information sources that would be utterly unknown to the average JW. Indeed, Stafford is no newcomer to the issues at stake when Witnesses interact with Christians on an apologetic level. He engaged in numerous discussions on America Online

during the years in which the book was in preparation.'
White exposes the fundamental flaws in Stafford's JW
reasoning on the Trinity (Christian Research Institute
Journal, vol. 21, No. 2, also vol. 21, No. 4).

The Christian Research Institute specialises in research
regarding sects, cults, the occult and issues of contemporary
theological and apologetic concern. 30162 Tomas, Rancho
Santa Margarita, CA 92688-2124 USA. Tel. (949) 858-
6100.

2. In England specialist help can be obtained from Reachout
Trust, 24 Ormond Road, Richmond, Surrey, TW10 6TH.
Tel. 020 8332 7785.

Also, Christian Information Outreach, Cobblecove
House, Buttway Lane, Cliffe, Kent, ME3 7QP. Tel. (01634)
222350.

3. Although JW emphasis on the importance of the name
'Jehovah' is not obscure, it is not dealt with here. A book
which deals thoroughly with this matter, and from a
perspective entirely sympathetic to the JW understanding
is the *Tetragrammaton and the Christian Greek Scriptures*
(1998). It is available from Christian Information Outreach
(above).

The book clearly shows how the Society's claim (that
the inspired Christian writers of the Greek Scriptures
restored 'Jehovah' to the text where previously *Kyrios* had
been written) is wedded to the matter of Christ's deity. For
this reason, the book and the booklet are ideal tools for
Christians to use in JW outreach.